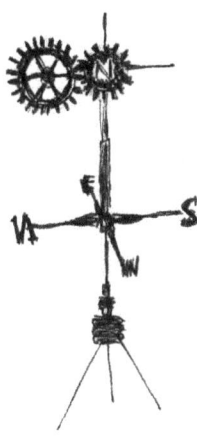

The Doors of Newmarket

Sue Anne Bottomley

ISBN: 9781958669204.

Book design by Karin Tracy

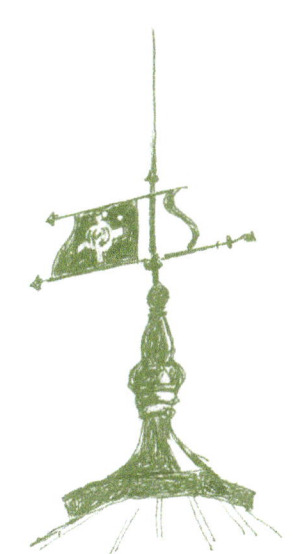

Introduction

There have been plenty of posters of doors. The most famous is surely a poster of the Doors of Dublin. The nearest example is another one—the elegant doors of nearby city Portsmouth, New Hampshire.

Newmarket also has enough intriguing doors to make an entire book of them. From the knock out brick one of the town library to old mill doors, churches, a former church now a live music space, a school turned into a museum, restaurants,stores, and private homes, Newmarket is a small town with an amazing array of diverse doors. Many have rusty hinges that have not opened in decades. The town is filled with double doors: two adjacent doors for two families sharing one building. Some have new stained glass fitted into an old doorway. Most are quite colorful: purple, red, blue, green, and yellow. These bright hues contrast beautifully with the deep grey granite and brick building materials.

Take a walk with me to discover the doors of Newmarket, New Hampshire.

Sue Anne Bottomley

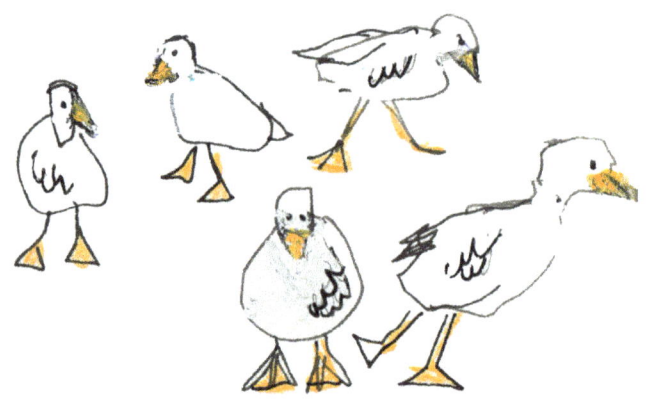

Timeline

- Traditional homeland of the Abenaki tribe
- Incorporated as a town in **1727** by English settlers from Massachusetts
- Center of the New England trade with the West Indies.
  Imports: whale oil, molasses, rum. Exports: timber and dried fish.
- Ship building along the Lamprey River for the Royal Navy.
  Twenty-one ships built during the peak year.
- Newmarket Manufacturing Company began in **1822**.
  Over time they built seven mills and 140 supporting buildings
  including worker housing and the library.
- Cotton fabric was produced before the Civil War, followed by silk fabric.
- Newmarket Manufacturing Company closed in **1929**.
- The town listed on the National Register of Historic Places, **1980.**
- The downtown listed as the Newmarket Industrial and
  Commercial Historic District, **1980**.
- The rezoning, restoration and reuse of the mill buildings began **2010-2012**
  by the Chinburg Company.
- The Cheney Company restored the last mill building, a warehouse
  at 4 Bay Road, **2019-2023**.

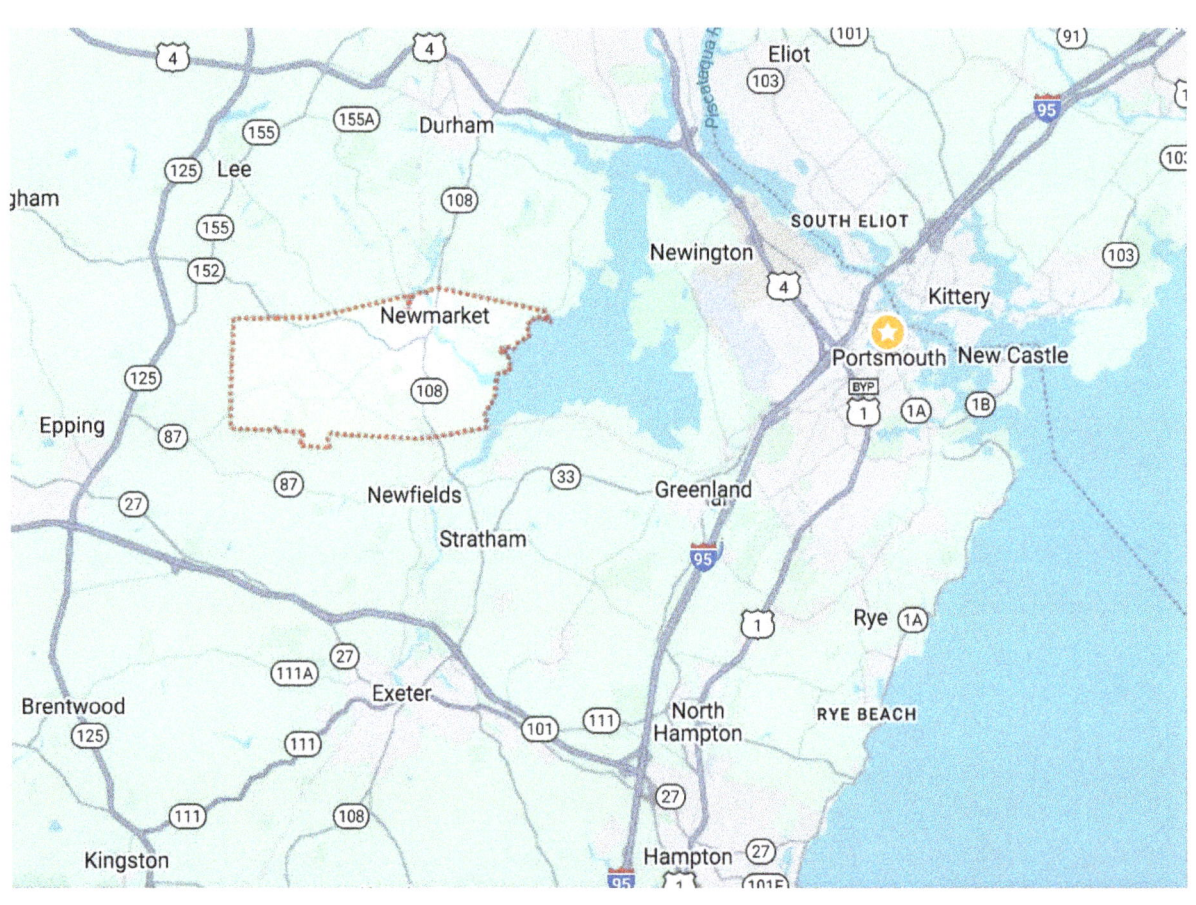

Key

1. Inkwell Florist, Main Street
2. Oak House, Main Street
3. Good Juju by Ceci, Main Street
4. Mill door
5. Mill door
6. Stained glass, private residence
7. Stained glass, private residence
8. Two-family, private residence
9. Ornate yellow door, private residence
10. Wing Itz, Main Street
11. Cracksculls Books and Cafe, Main Street
12. Newmarket Community Church, Main Street
13. St. Mary's Catholic Church, Main Street
14. Newmarket Town Hall, Main Street
15. Sprinkled on Main, Basil Leaf, Main Street
16. Newmarket Engine House, Main Street
17. Rockingham Junction Railroad Station
18. Dove cote, Rockingham Ballroom
19. Tequila Rae's, 5 Monkeys Tattoo, Main Street
20. Jonny Boston's, Main Street
21. The Riverworks, Main Street
22. Roots Local Café, interior door, Main Street
23. The Big Bean, Main Street
24. Garage, private property
25. The Willey House, Main Street
26. Art Nouveau door, Main Street
27. Purple door, private residence
28. The Tipsy Tabby, Main Street
29. The Durham Book Exchange, Chinburg courtyard
30. Elements of Steel, Main Street
31. Four garages, private property
32. The Stone Church Music Club, Granite Street
33. Newmarket Historical Society, Granite Street

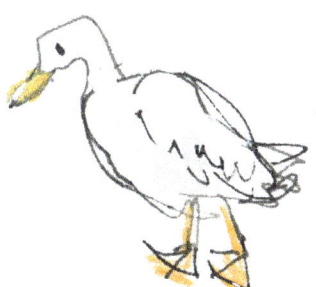

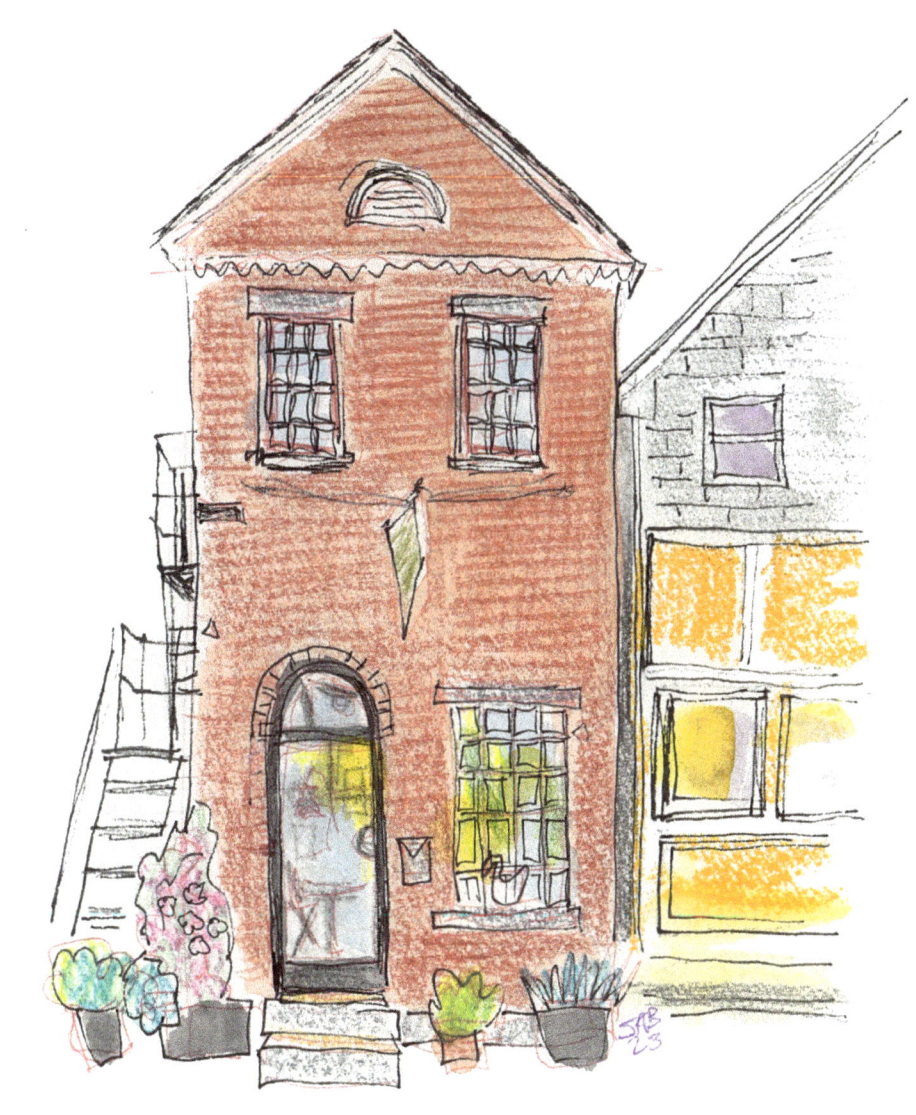

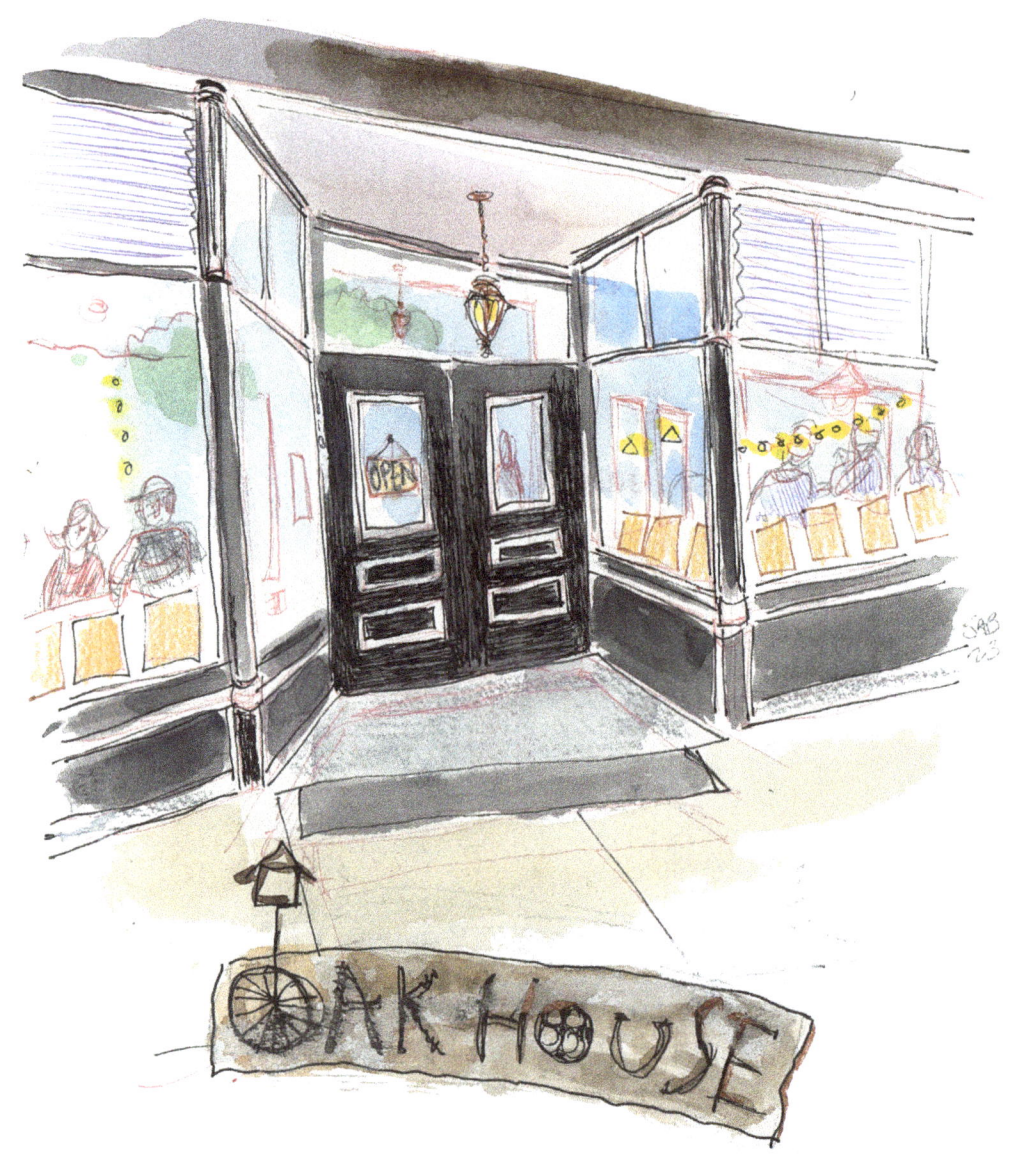

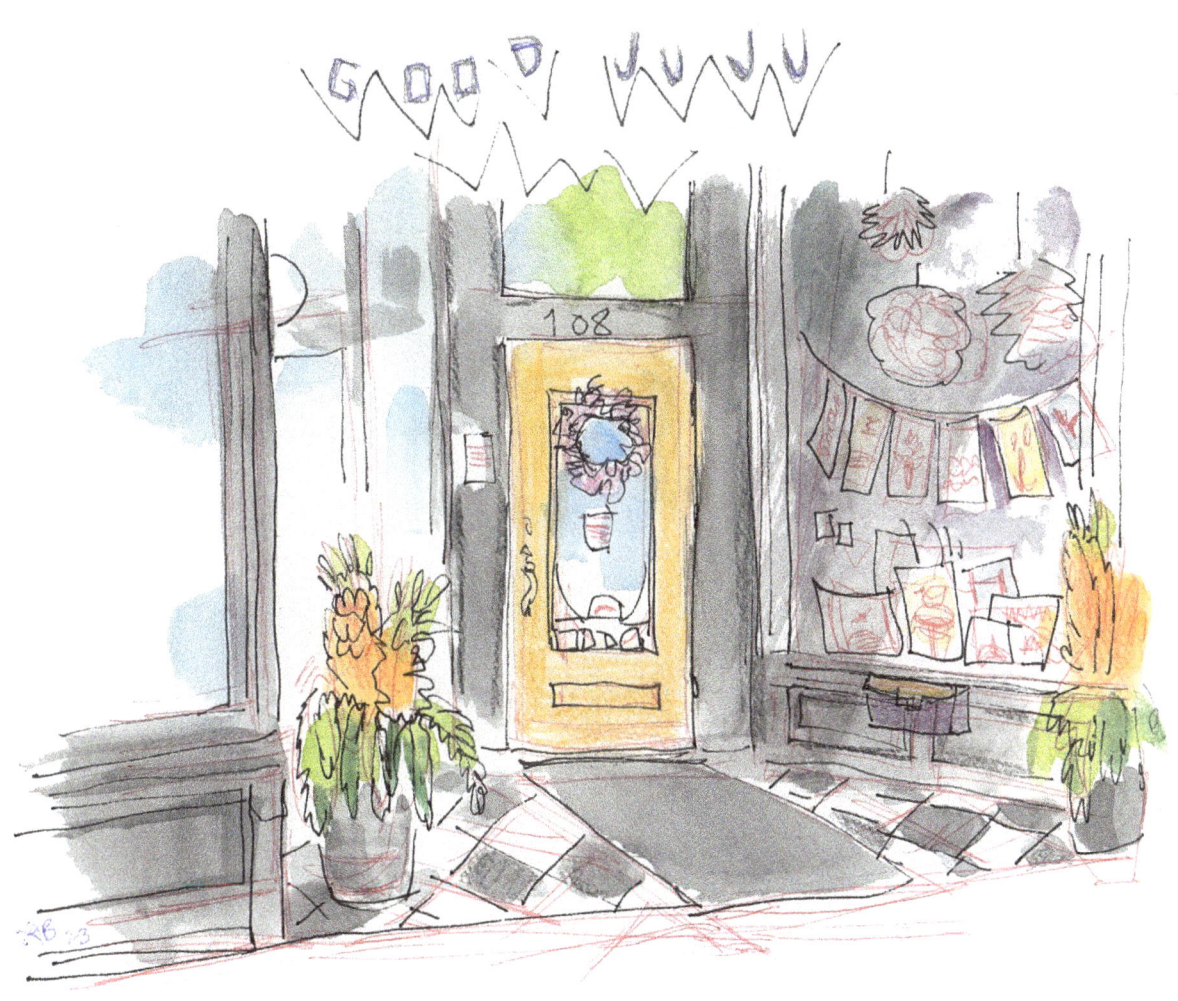

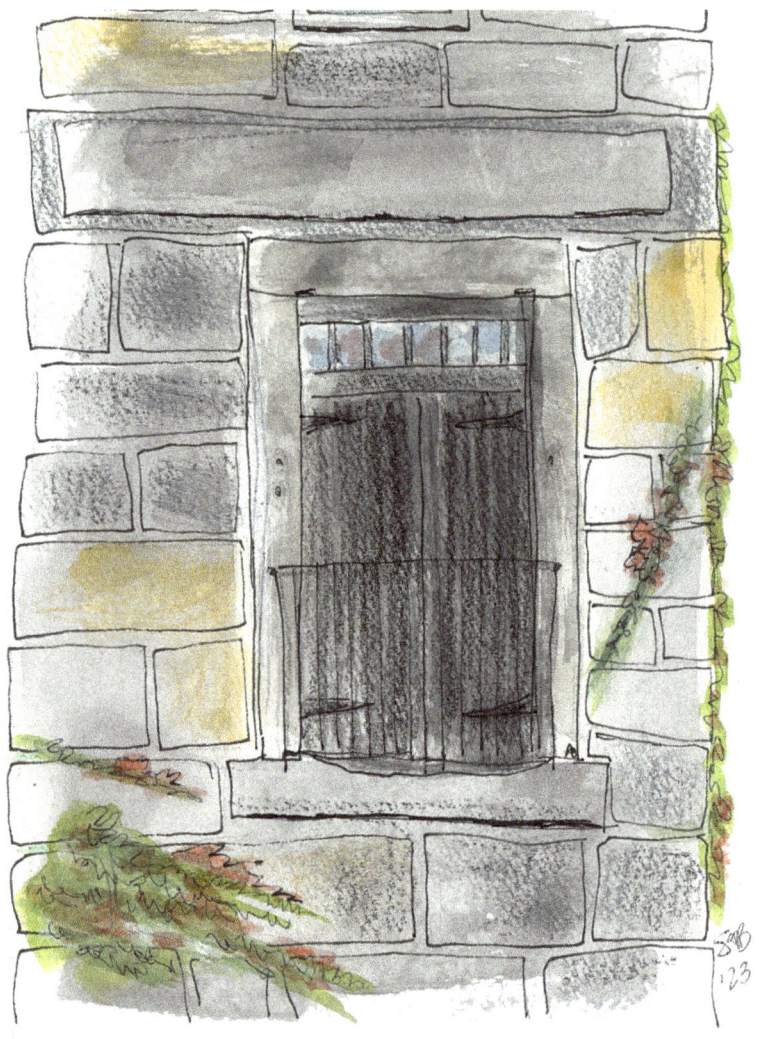

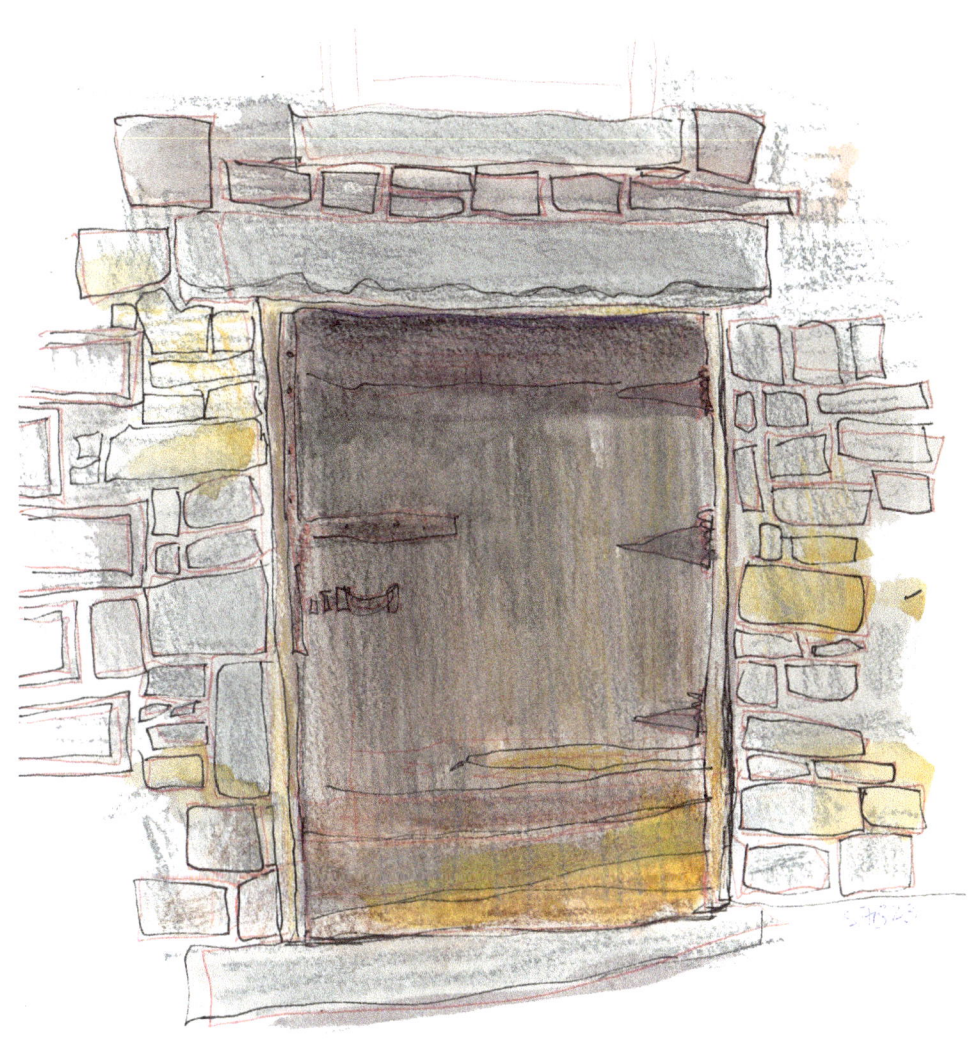

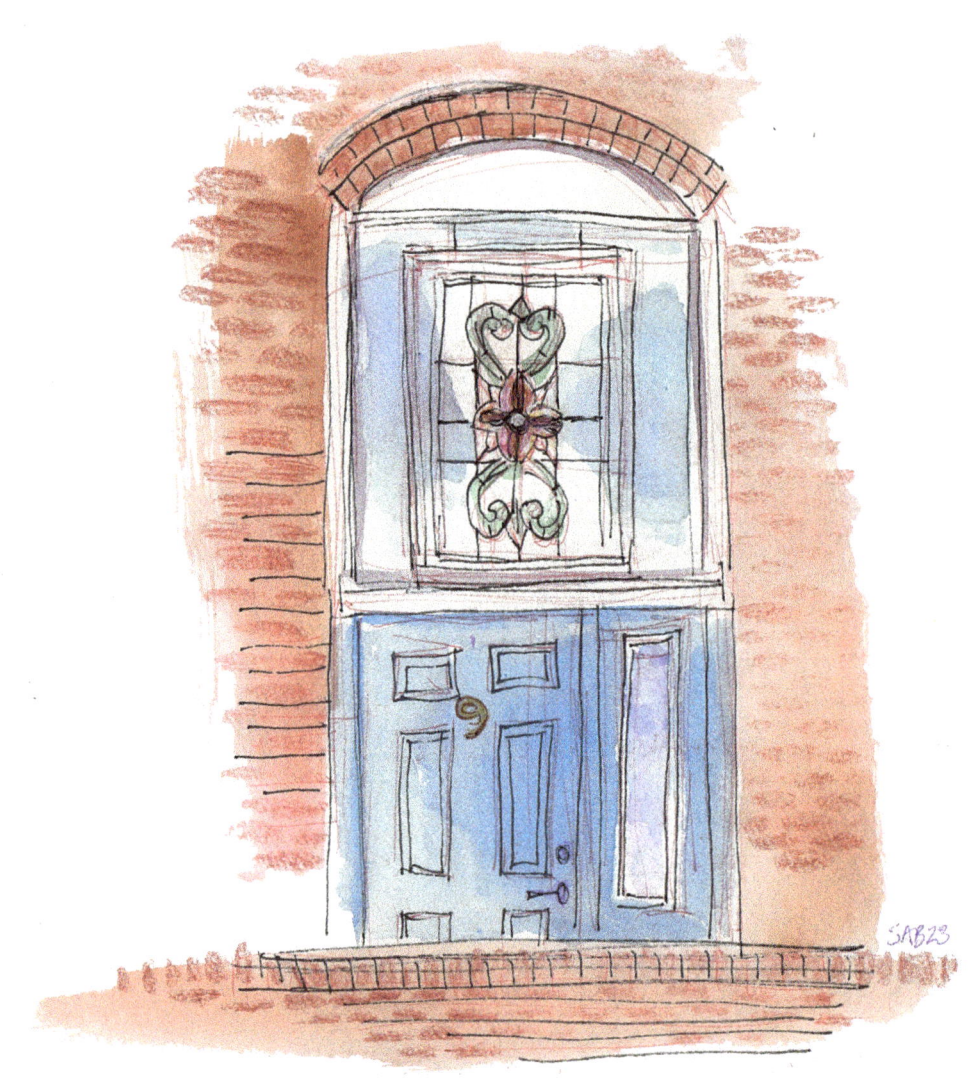

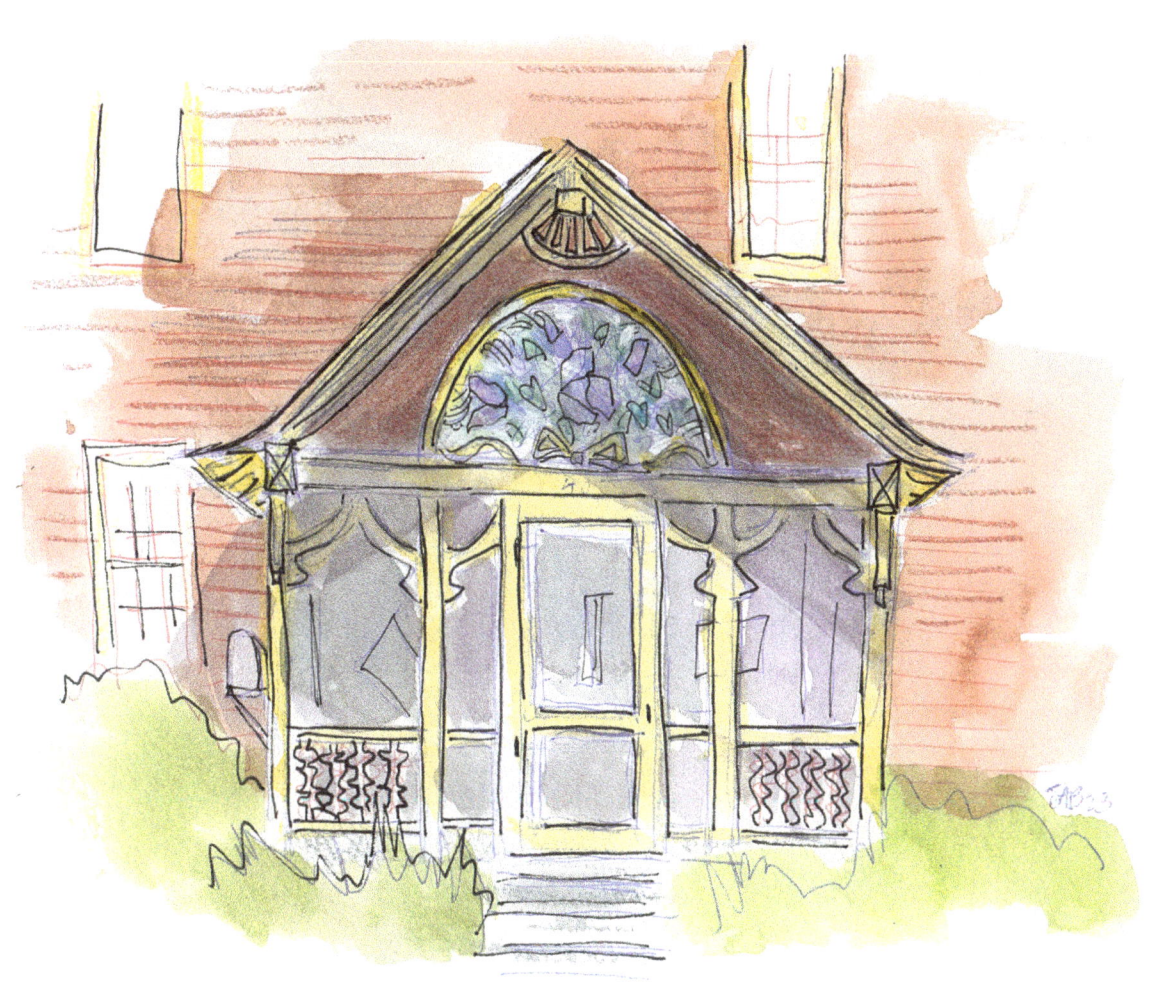

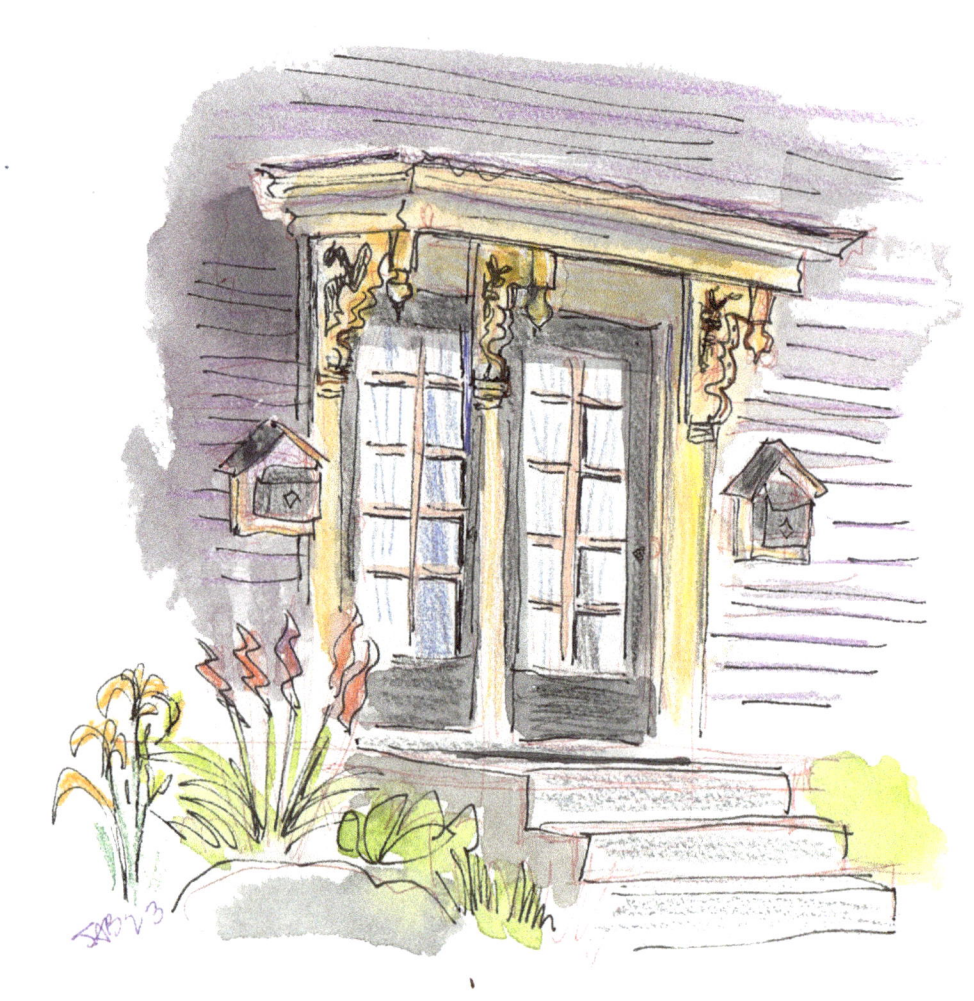

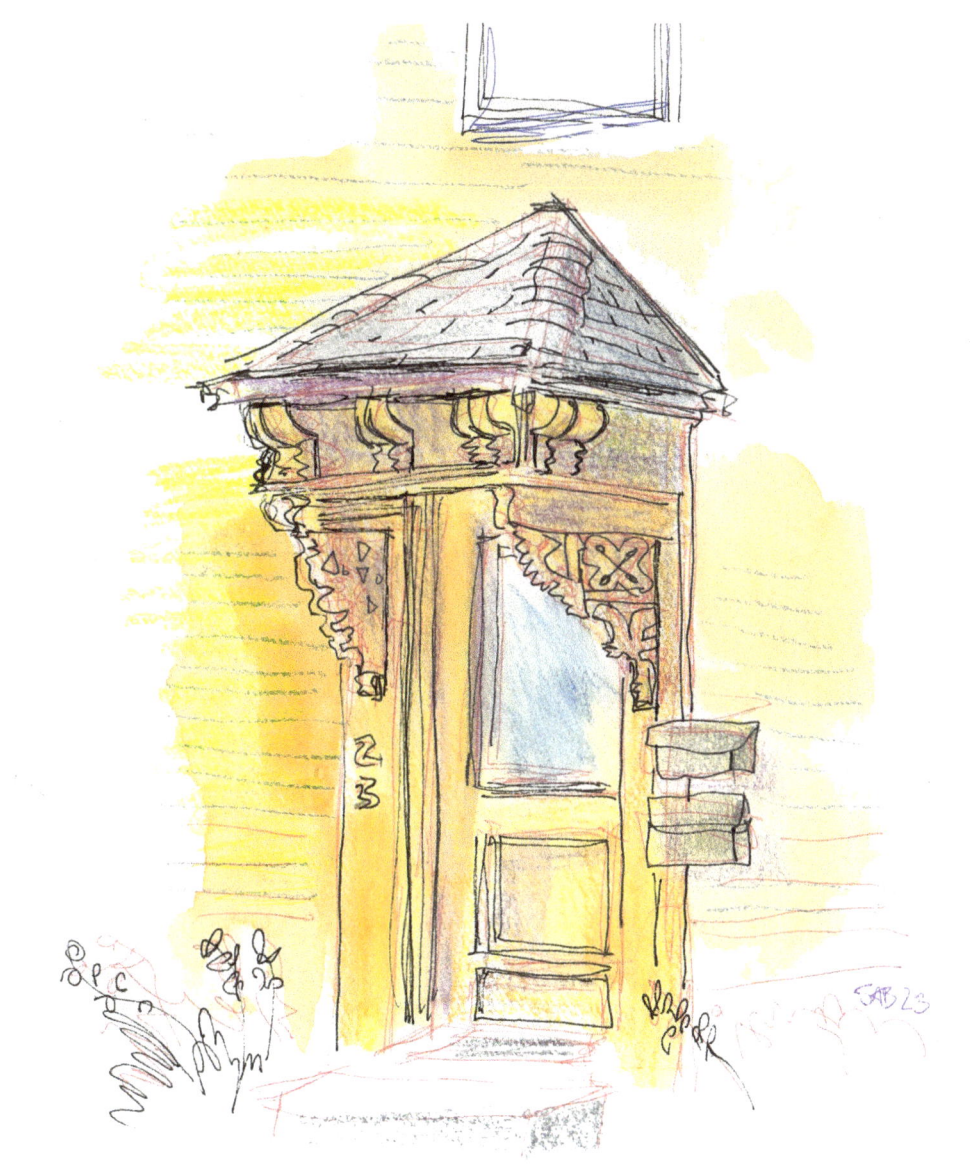

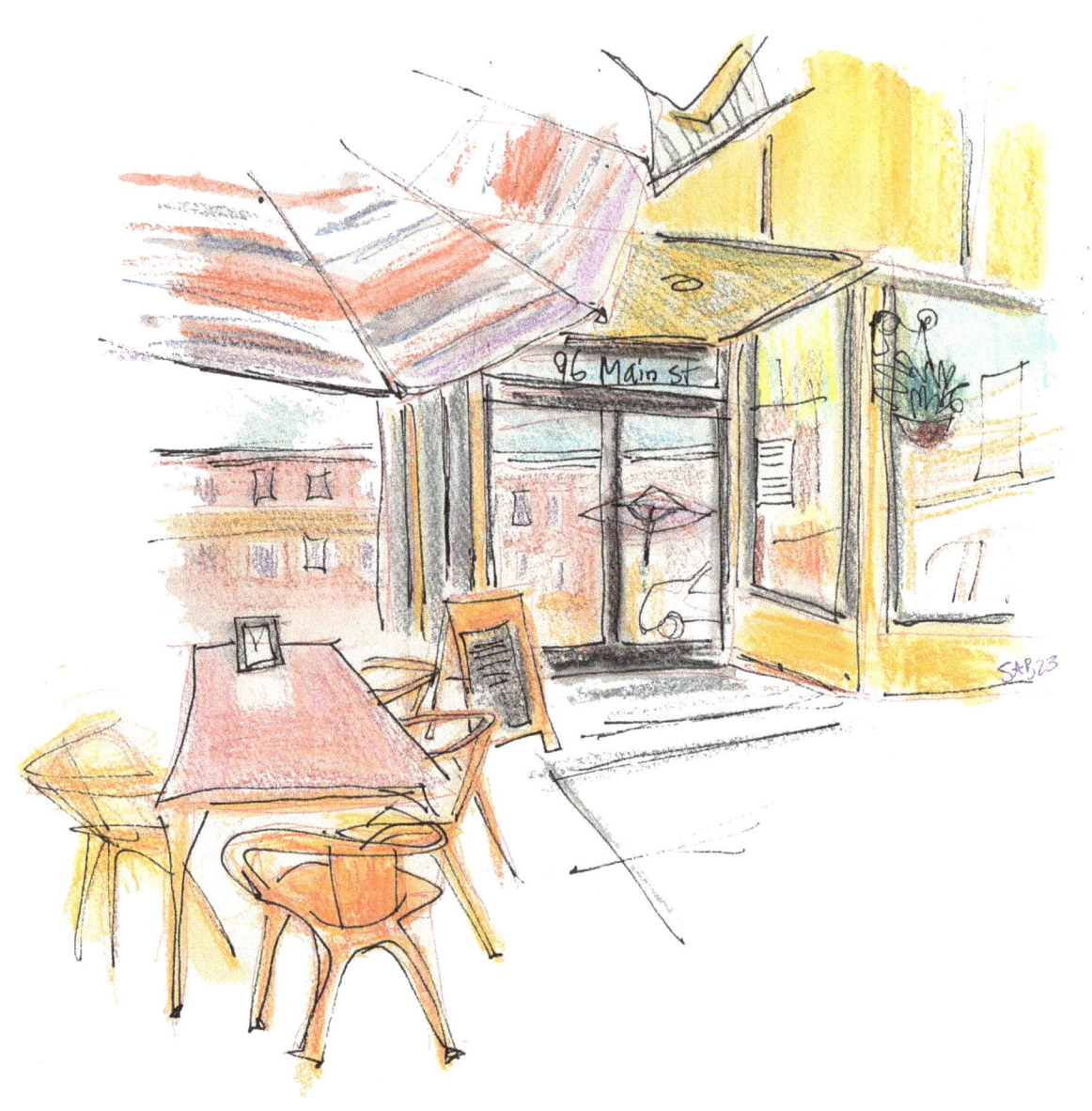

10

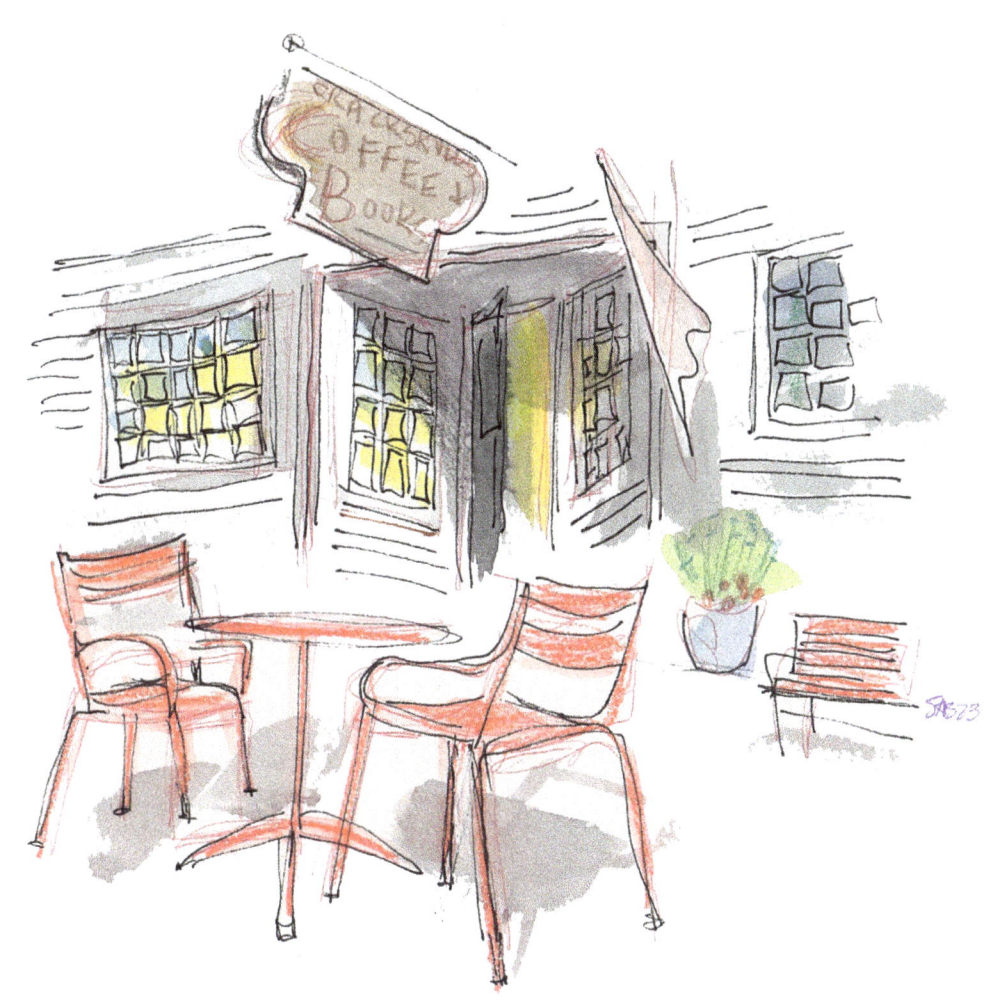

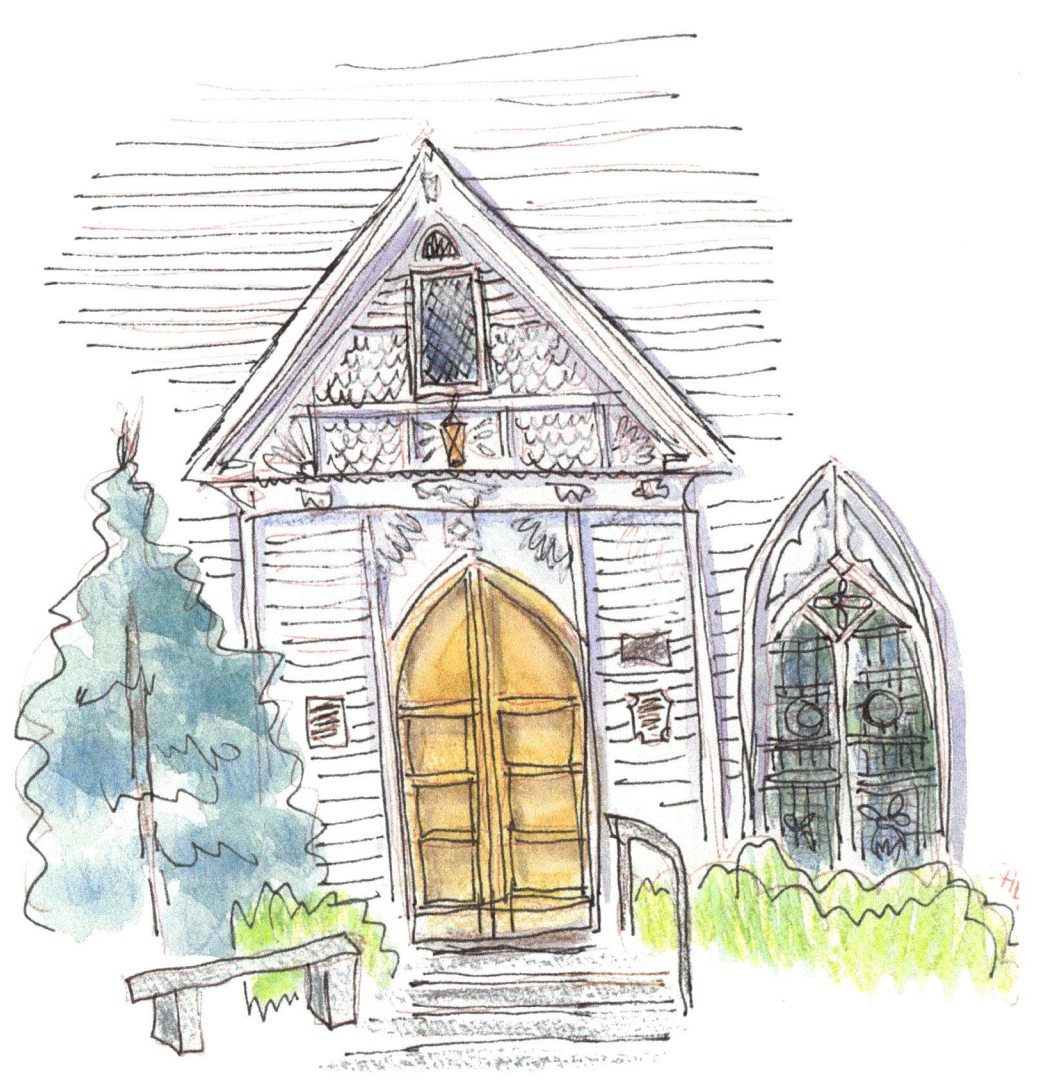

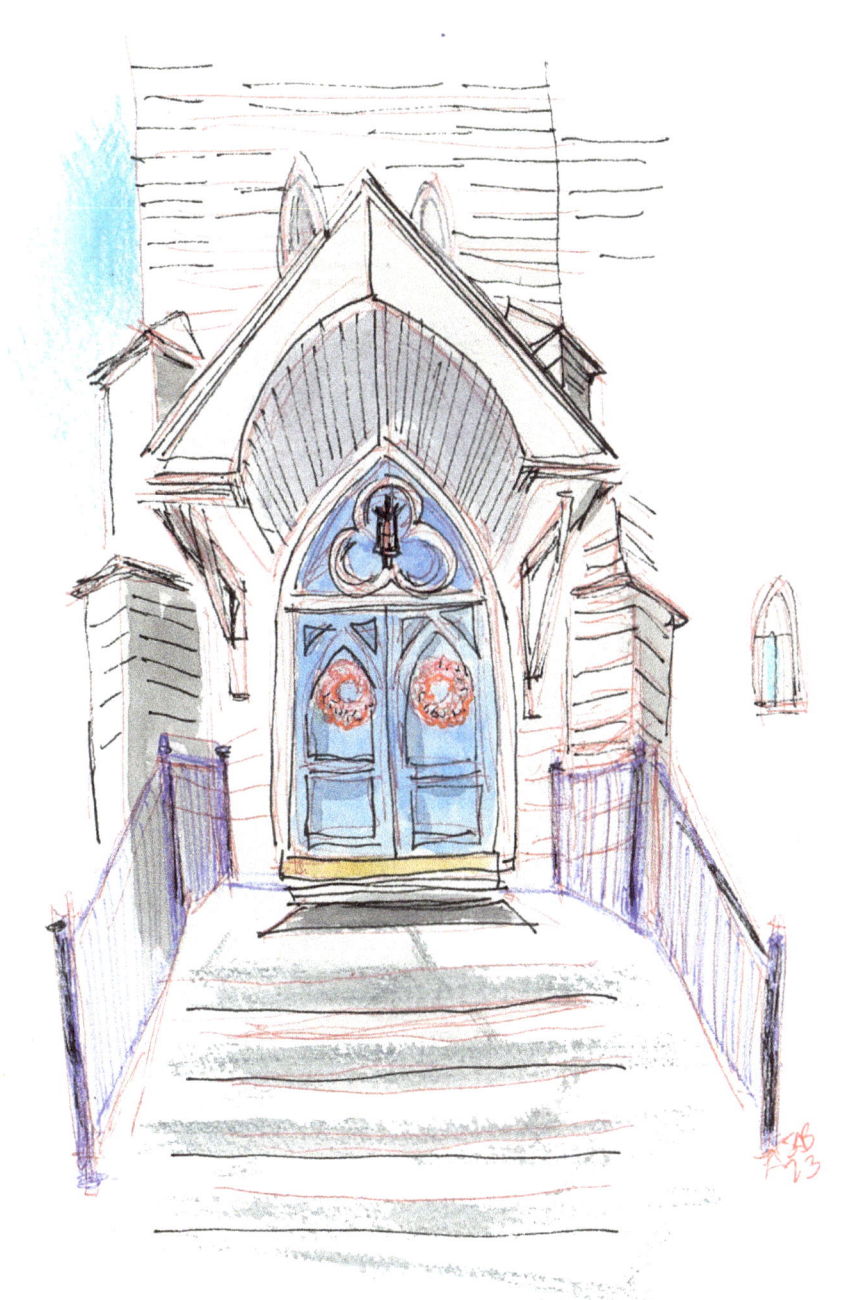

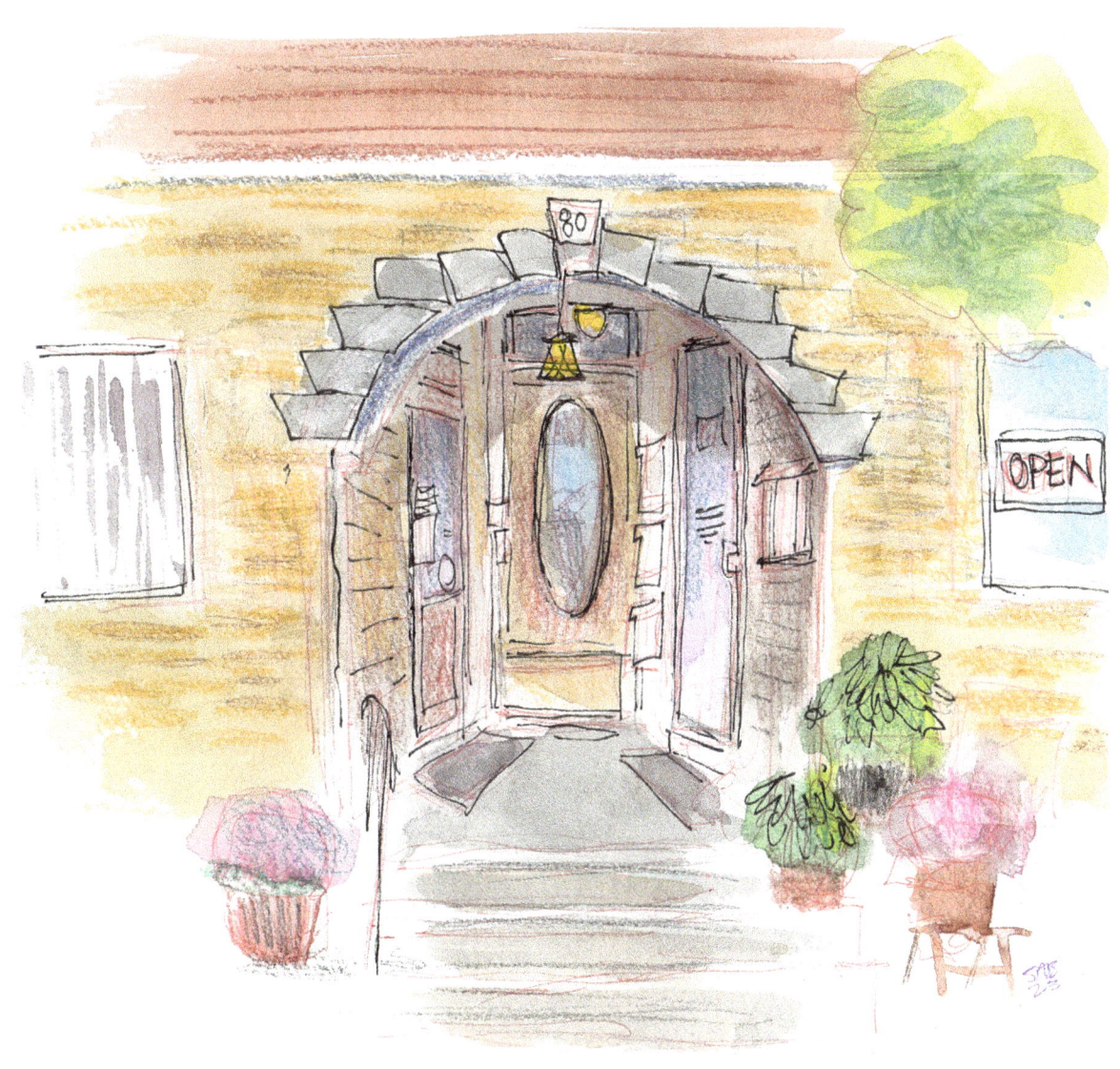

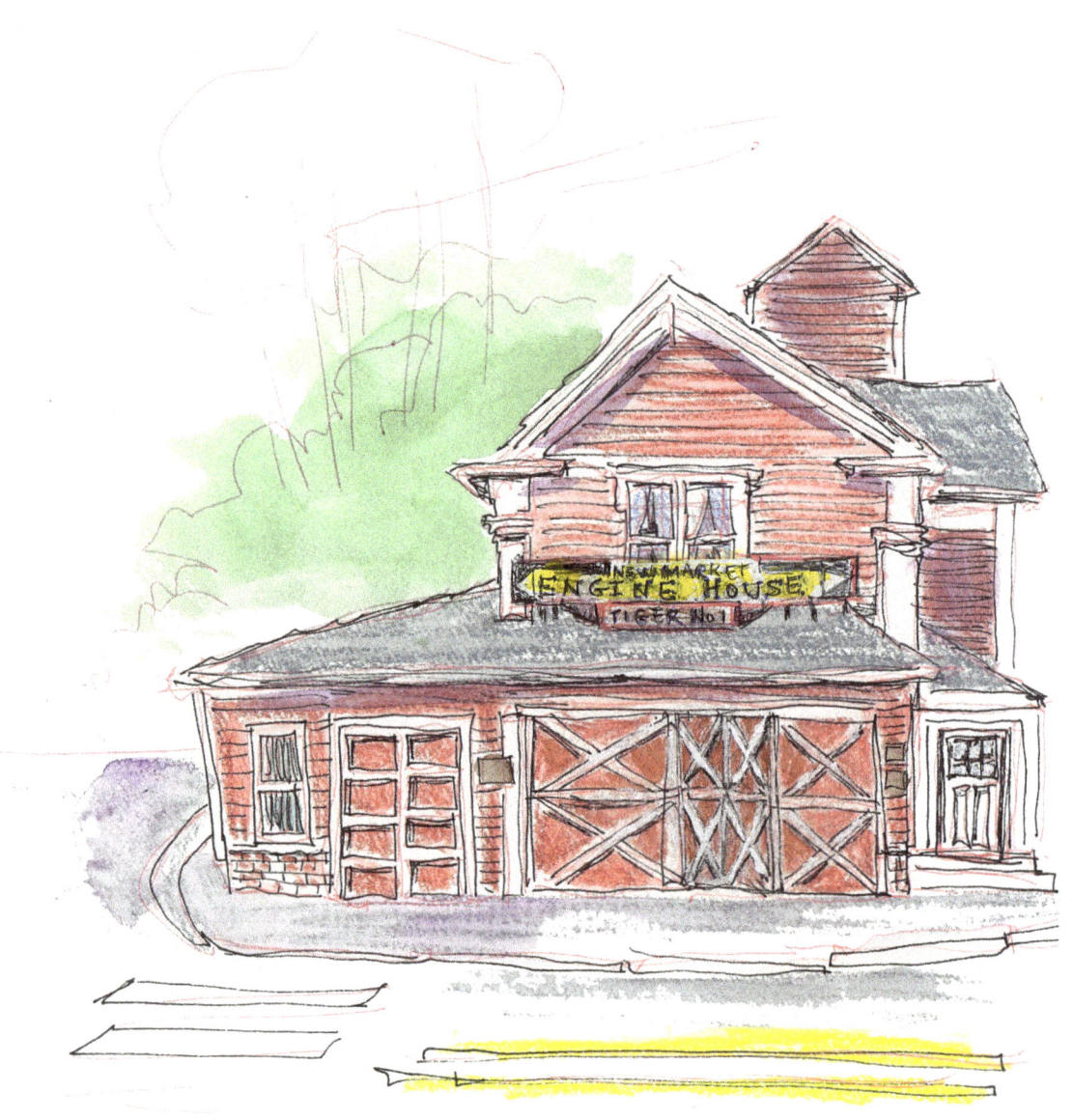

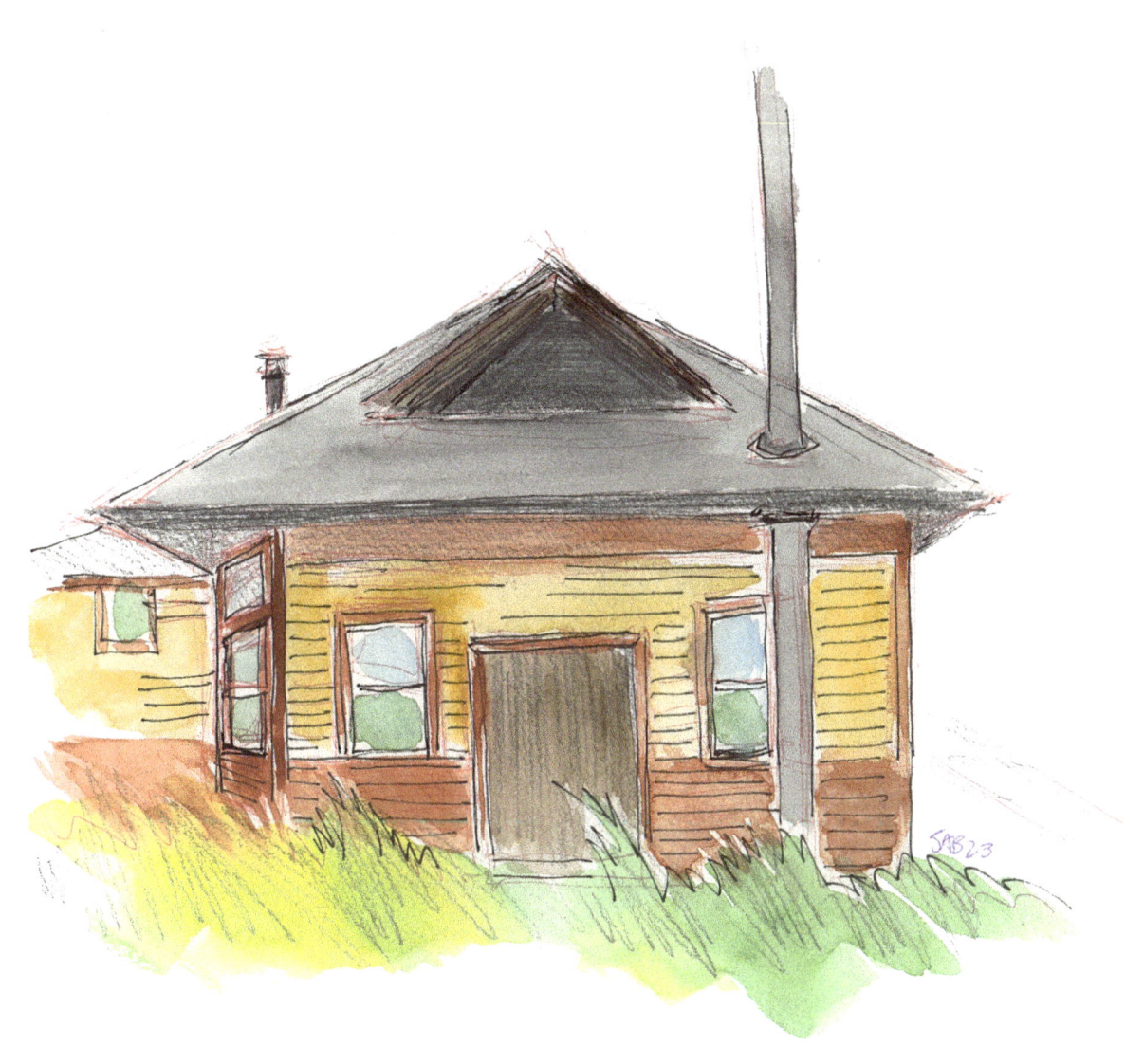

17

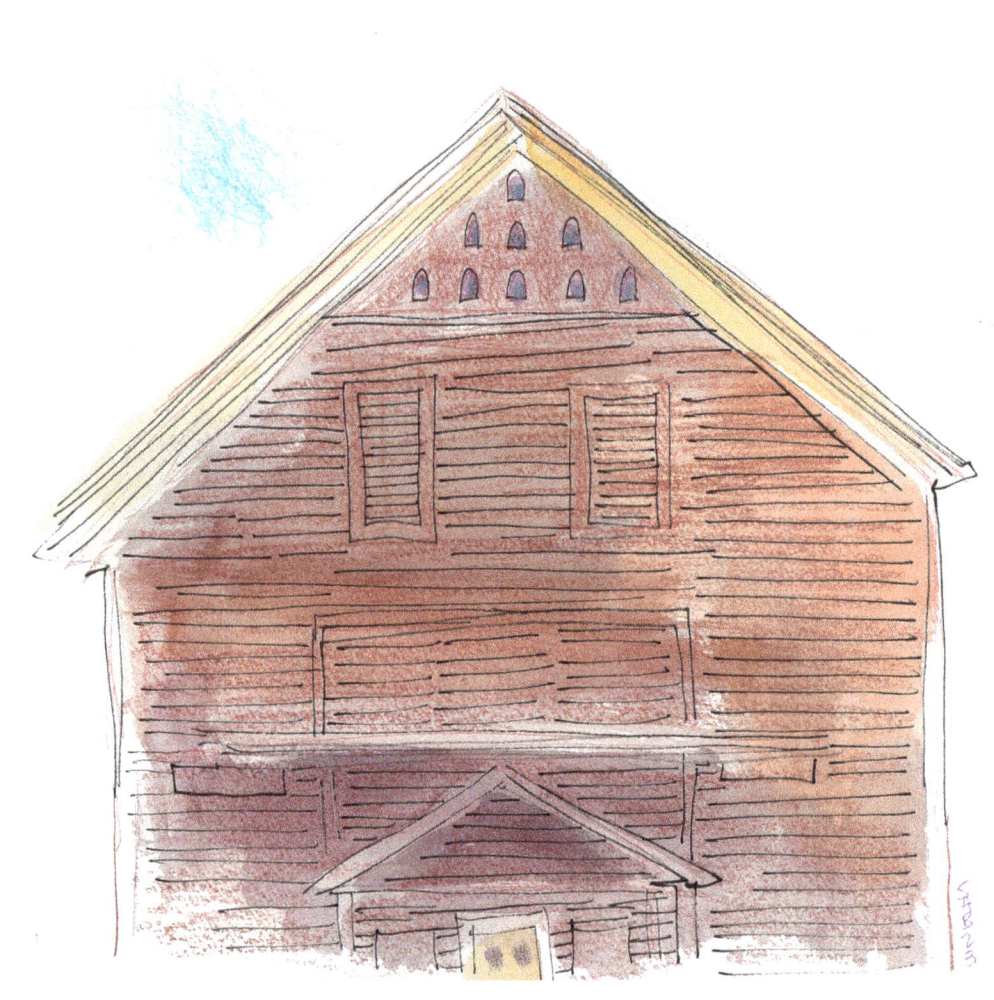

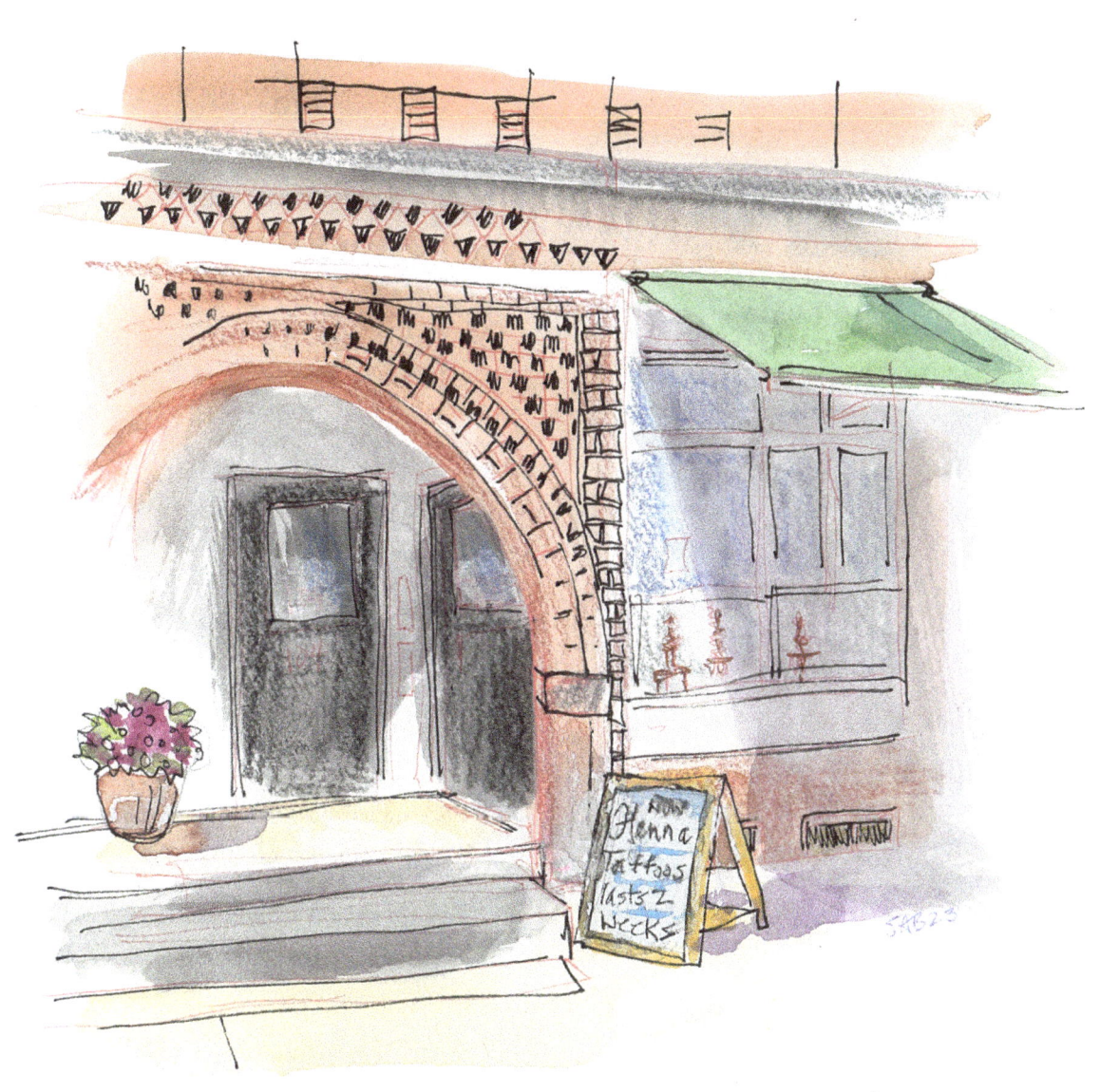

The sign reads: "NEW Henna Tattoos lasts 2 weeks"

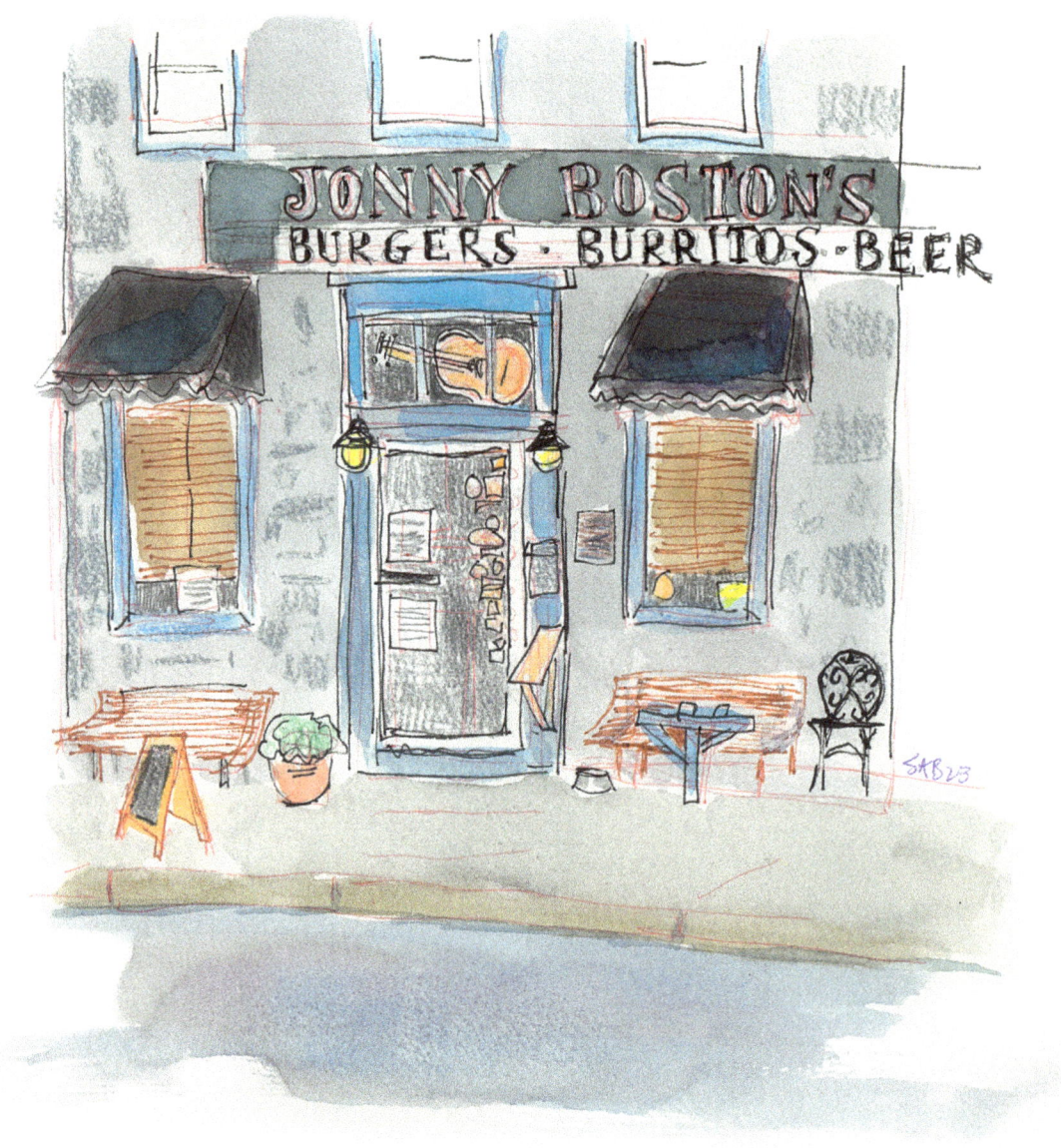

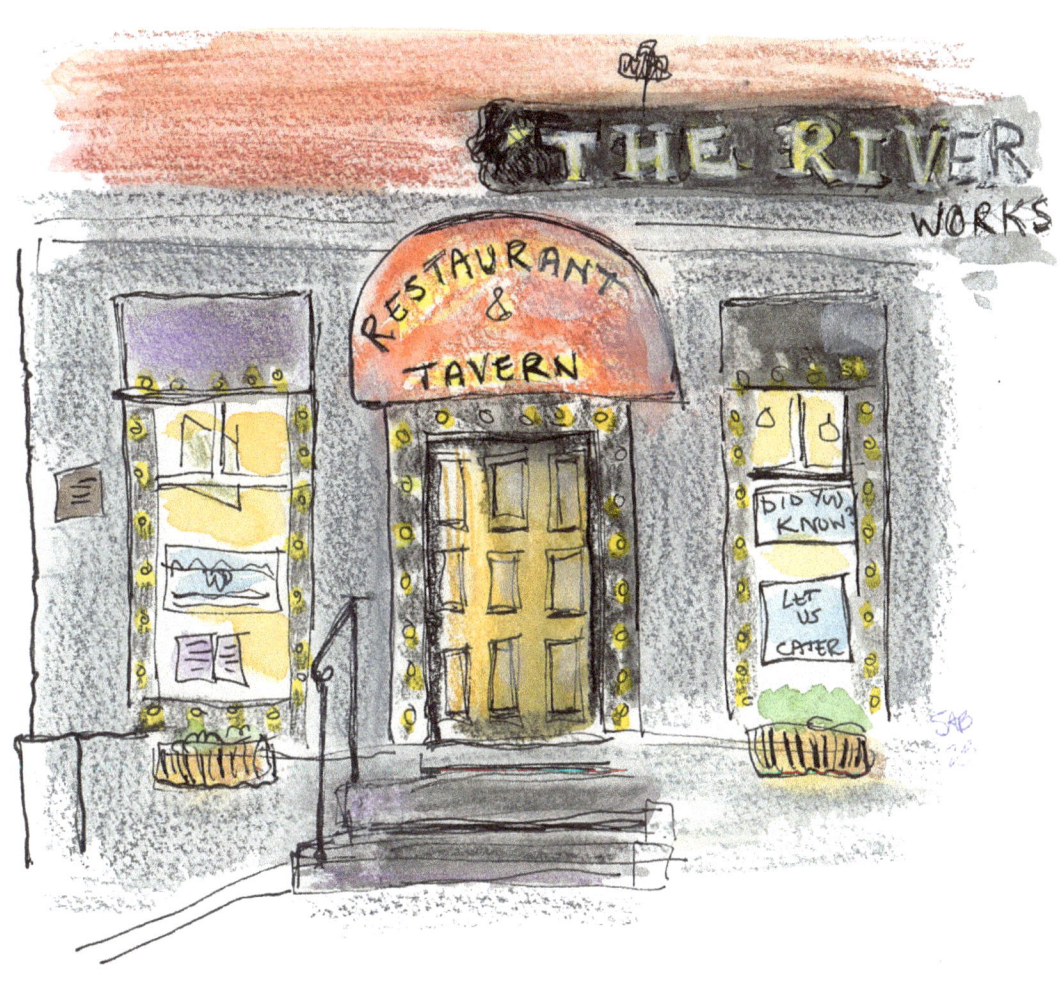

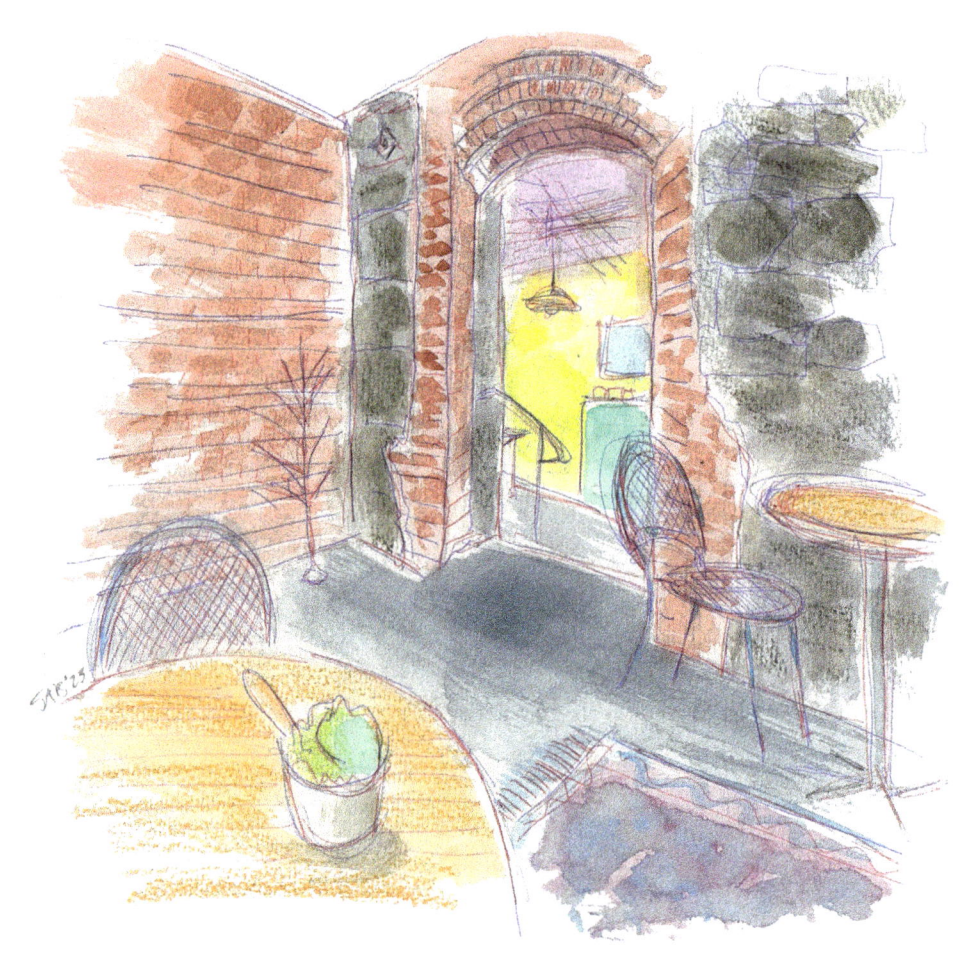

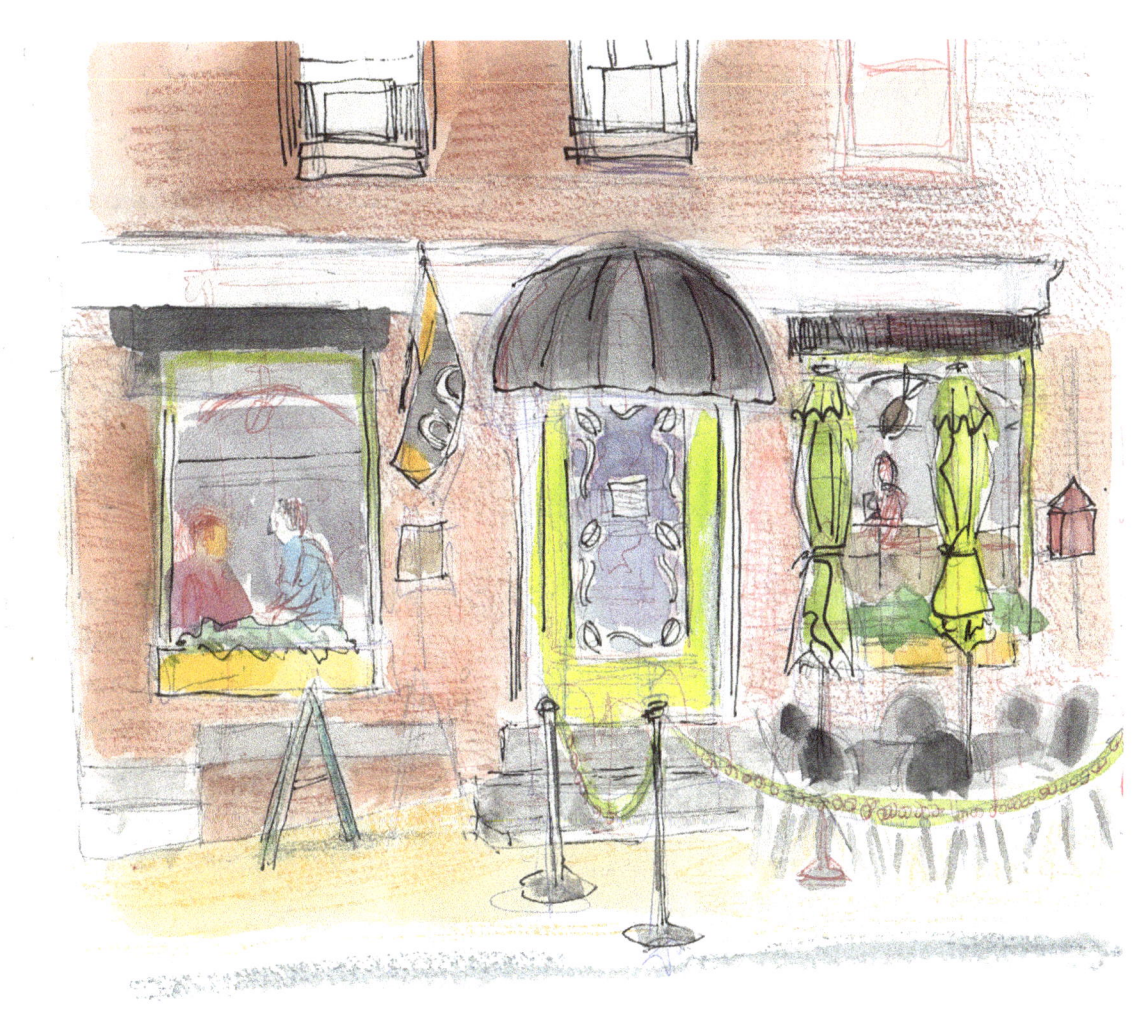

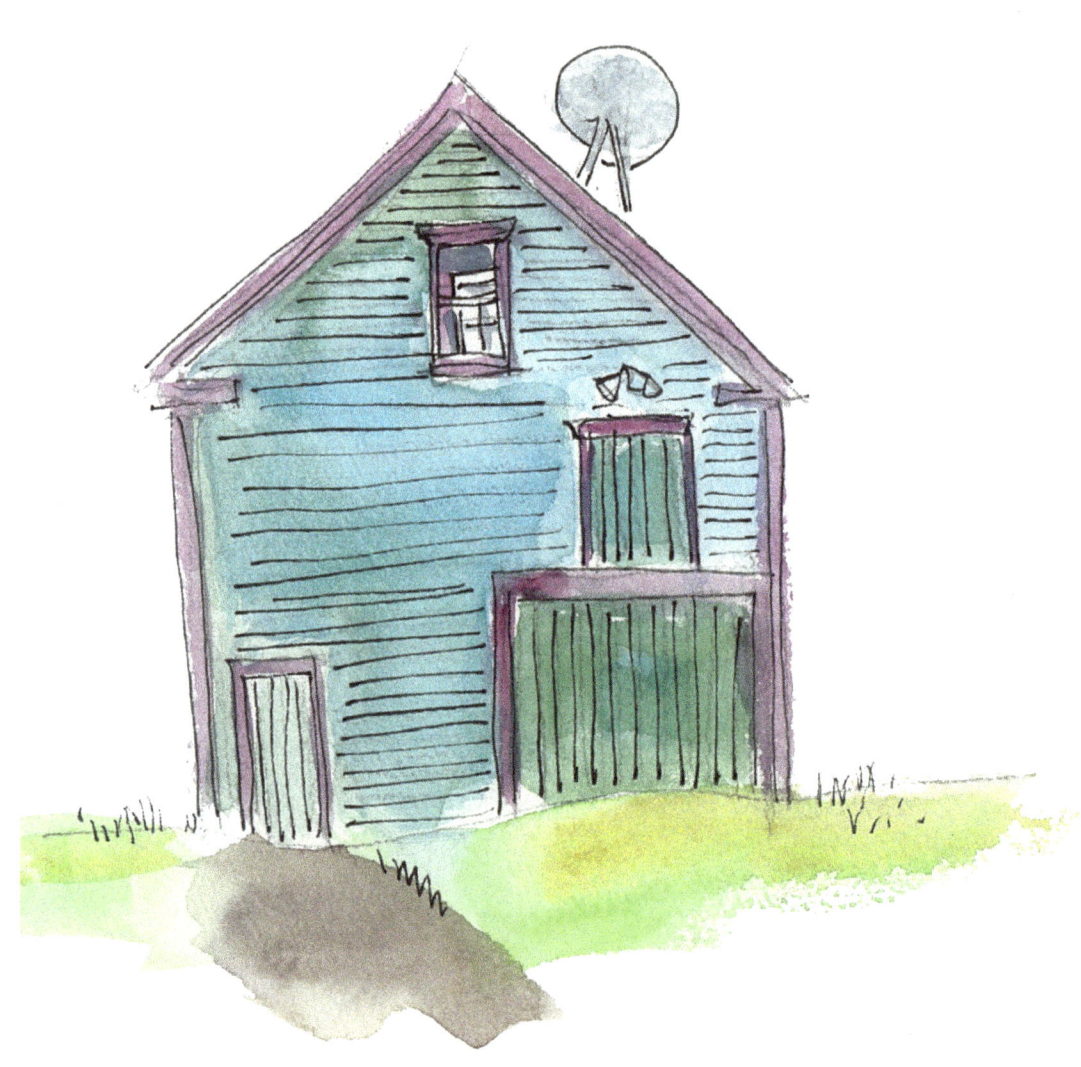

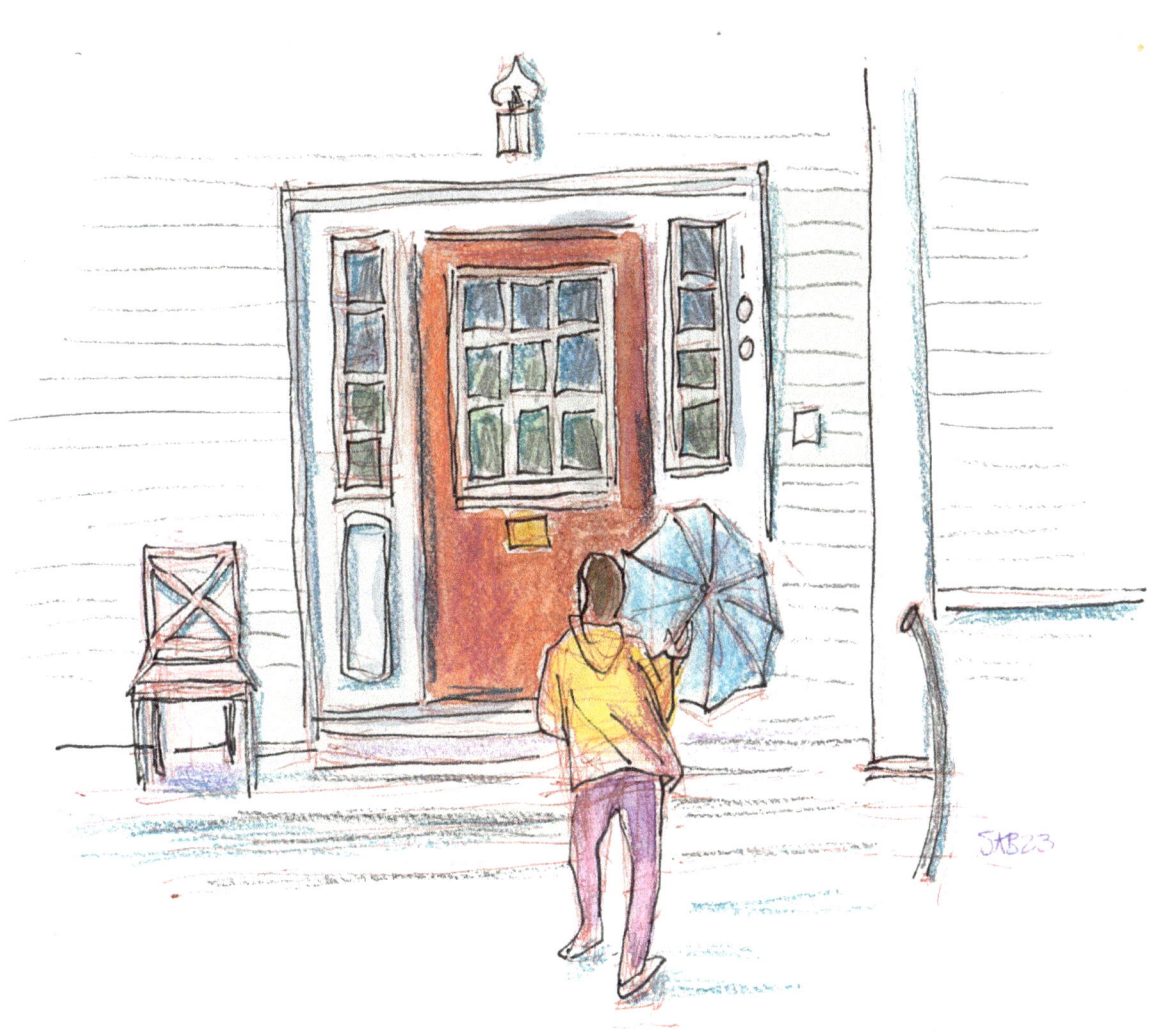

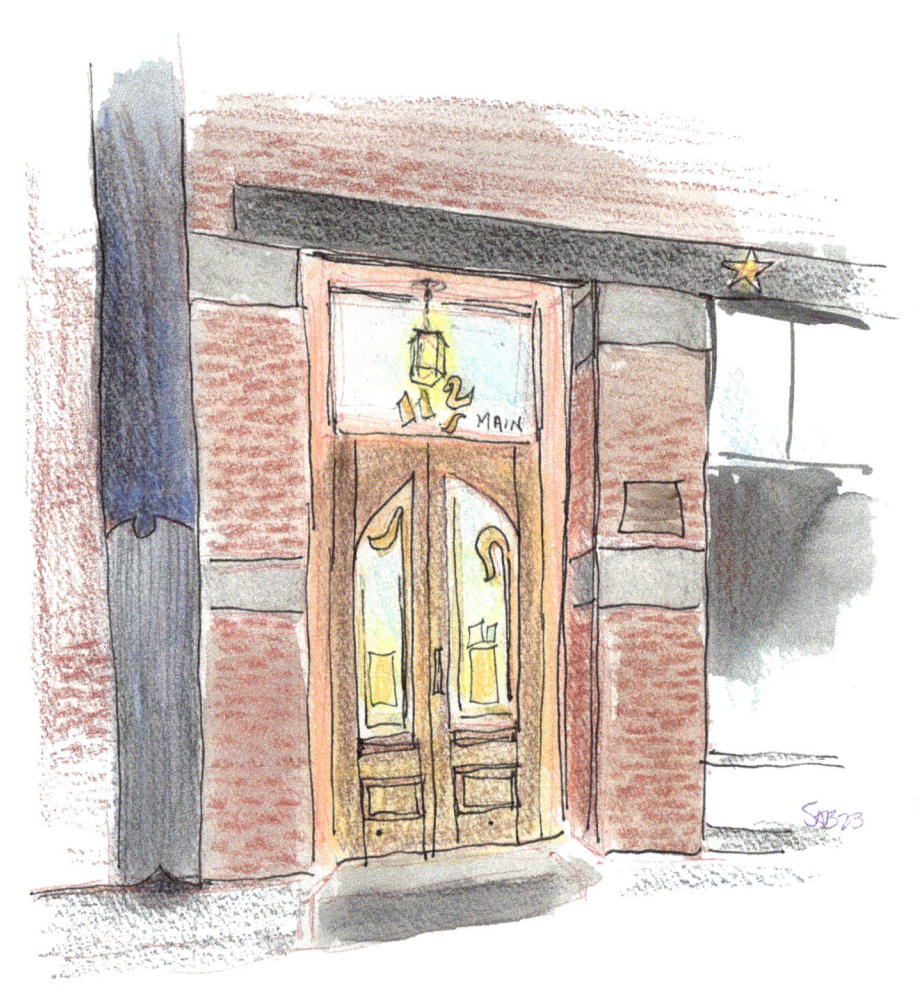

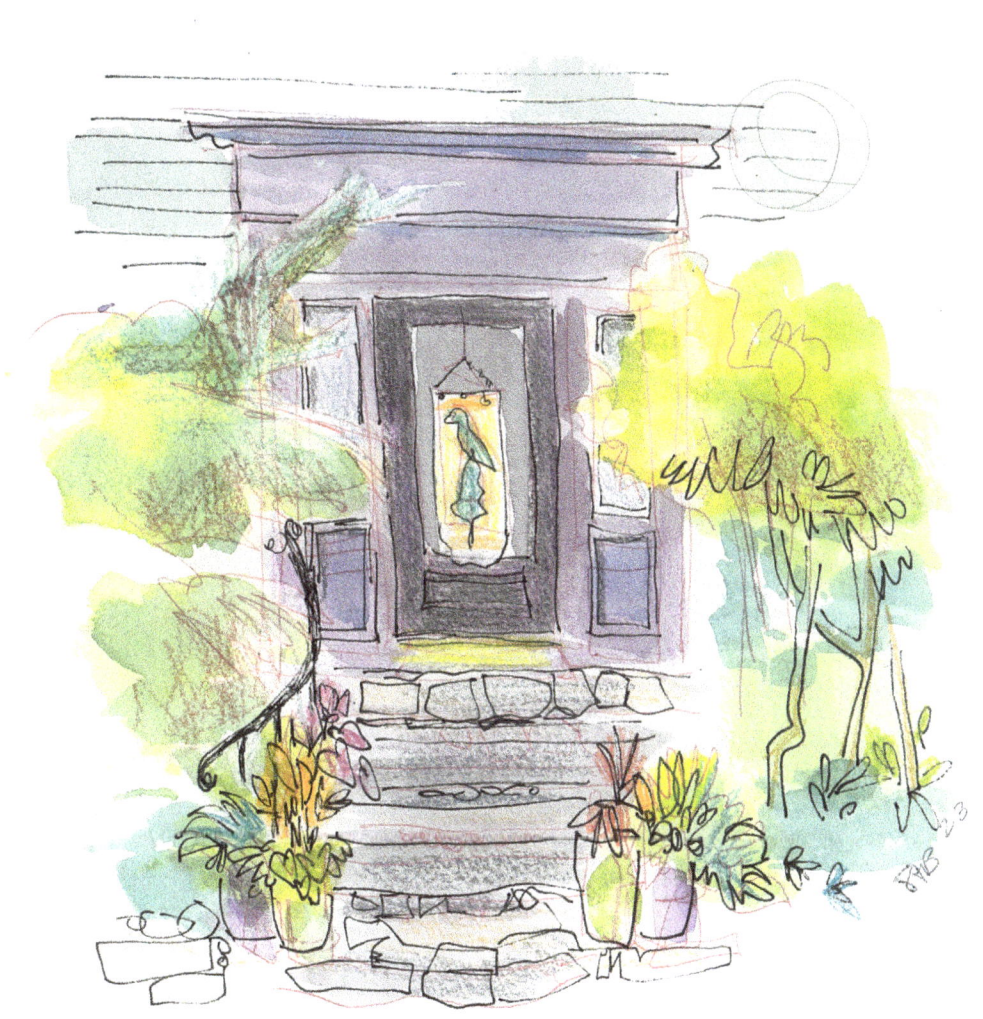

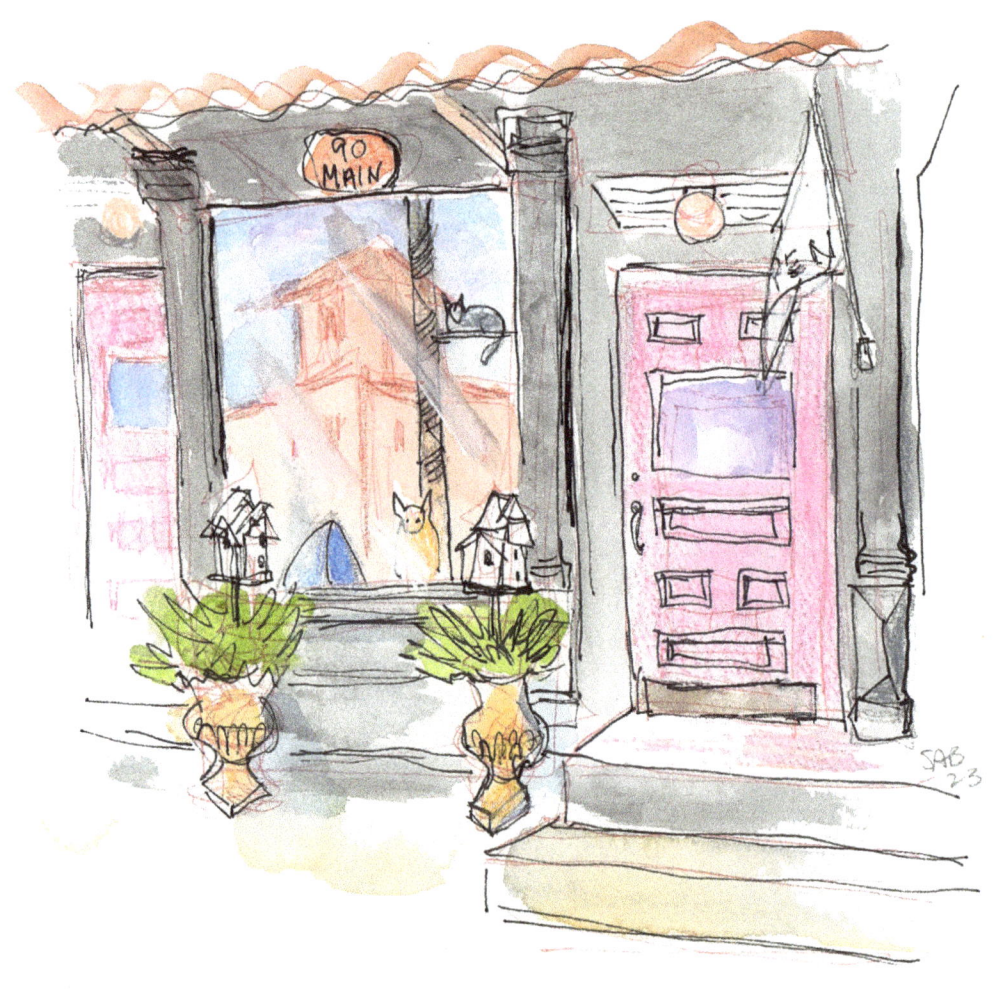

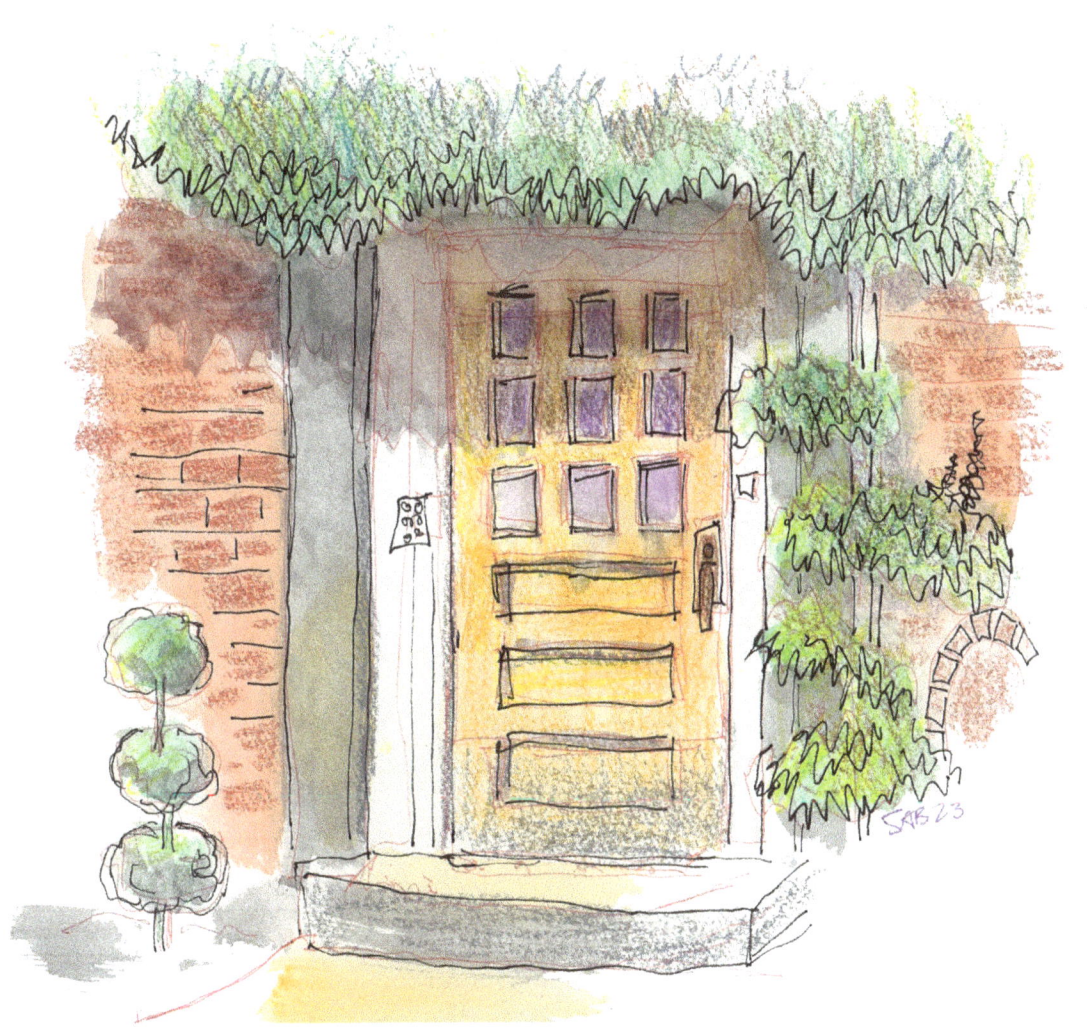

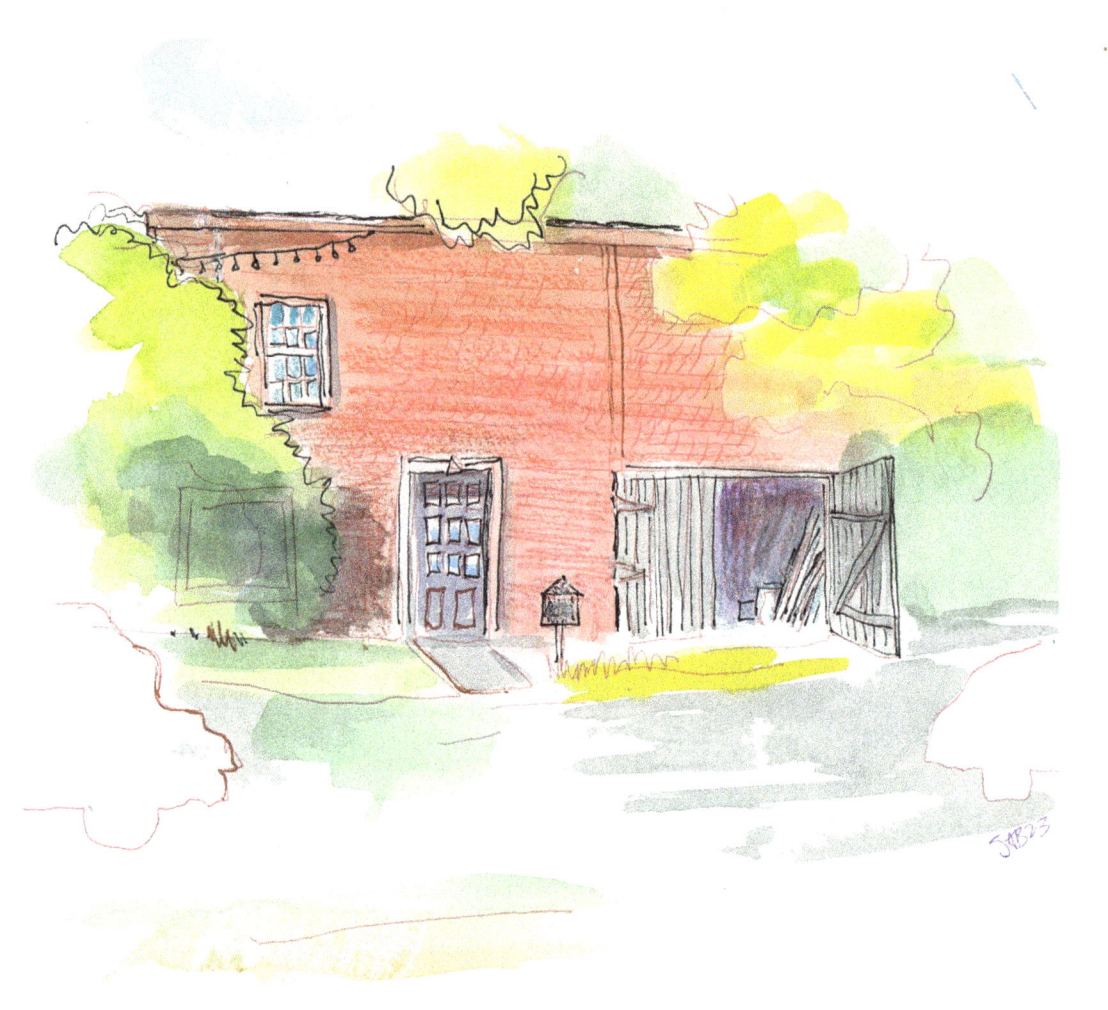

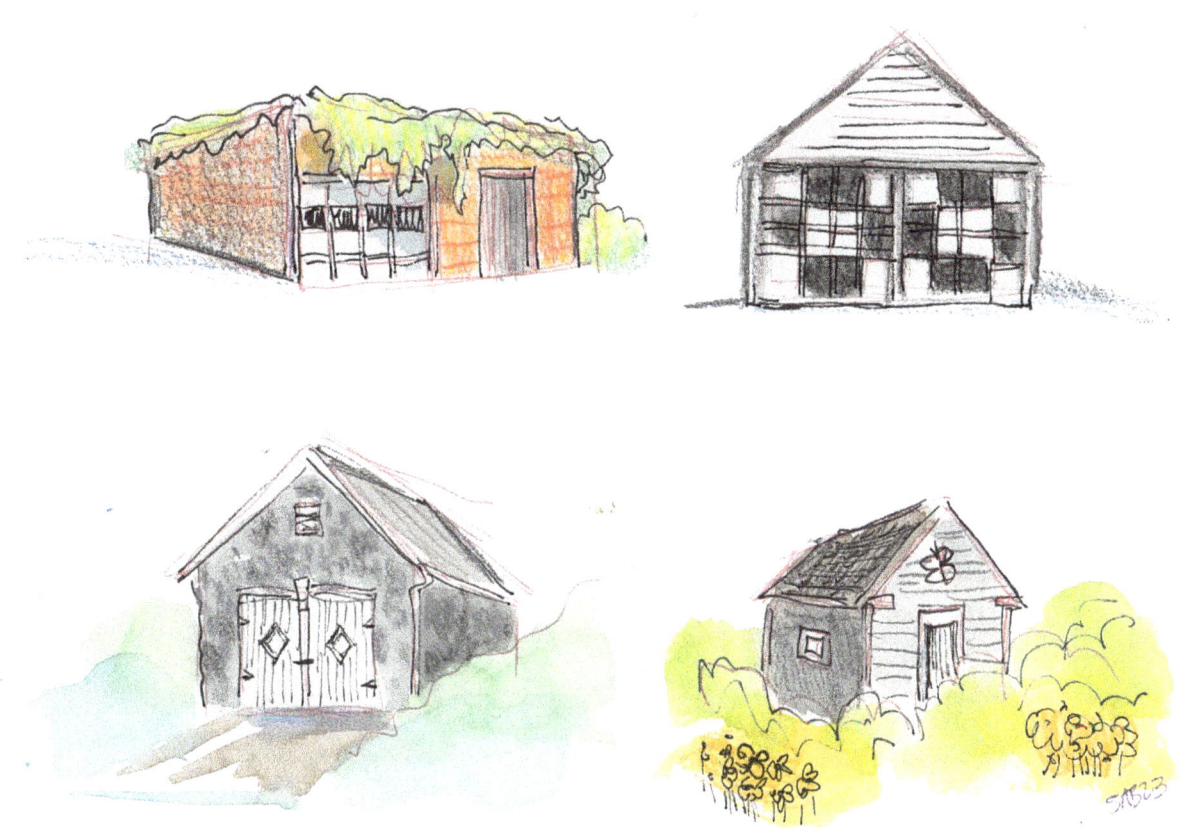

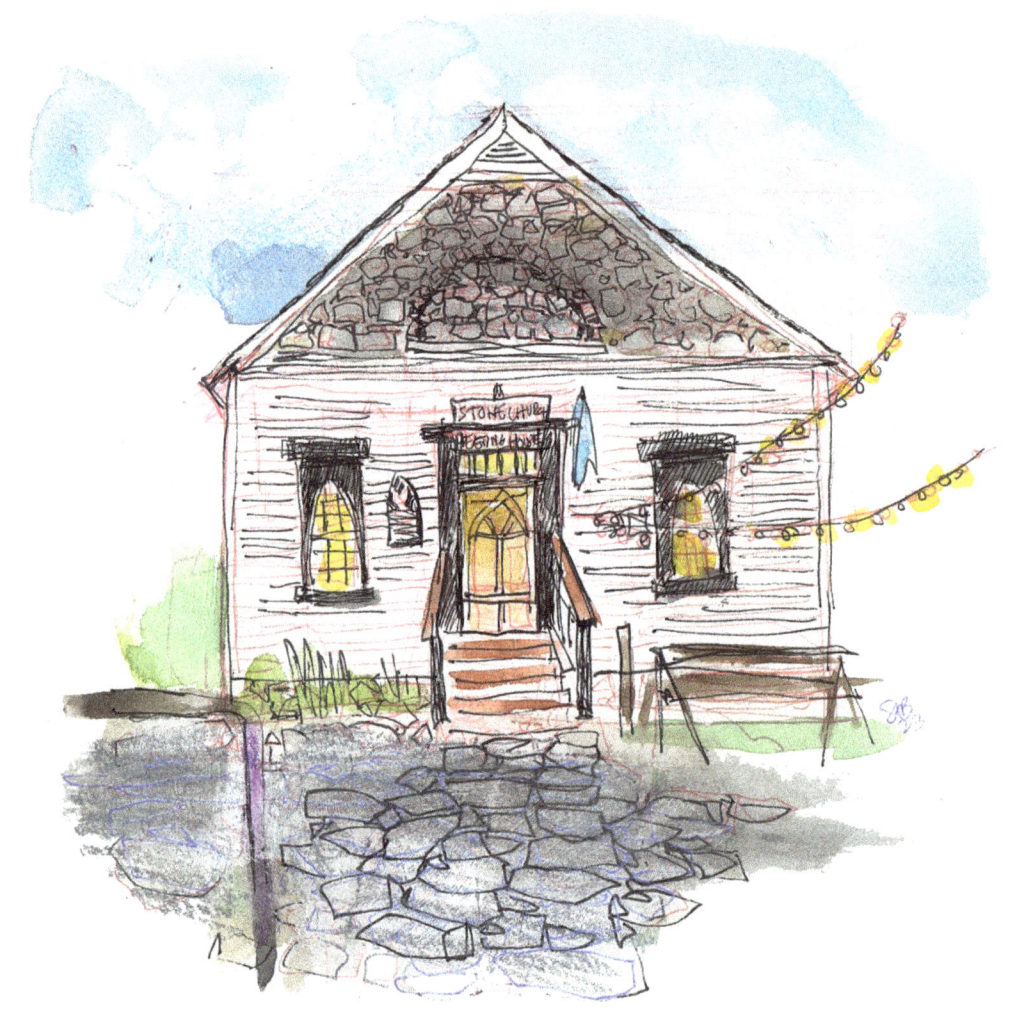

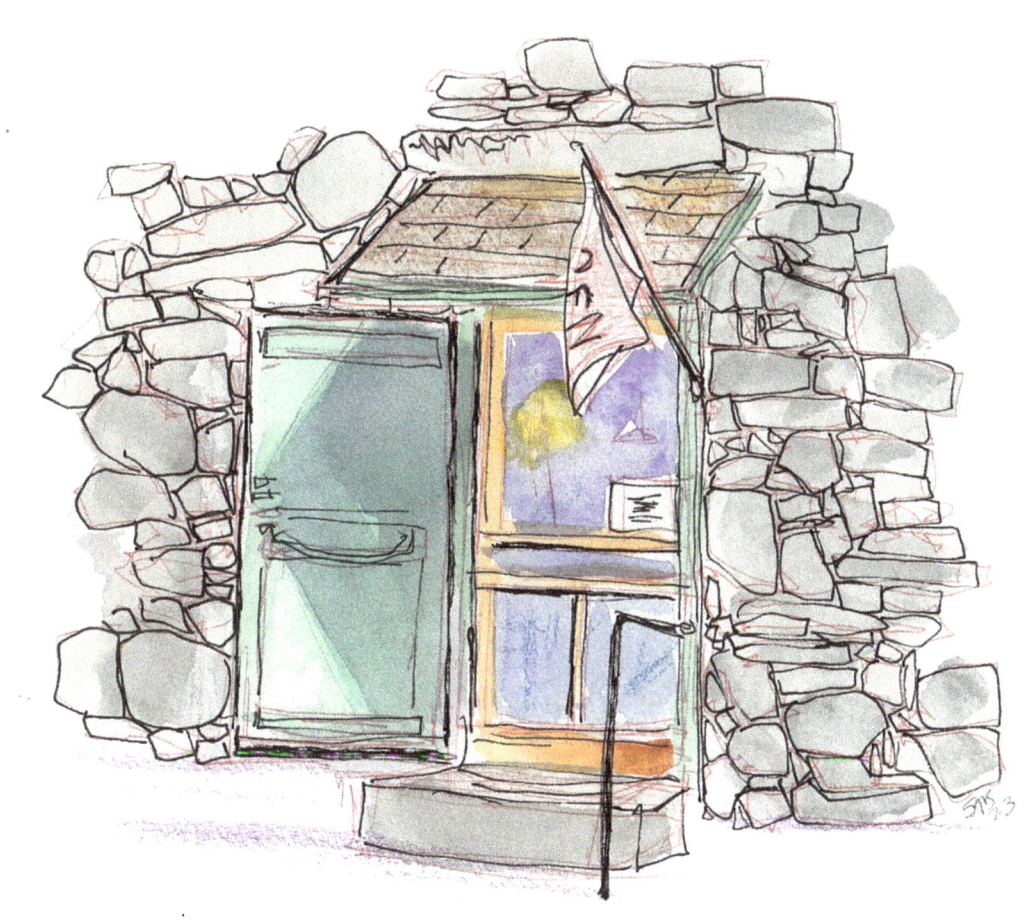

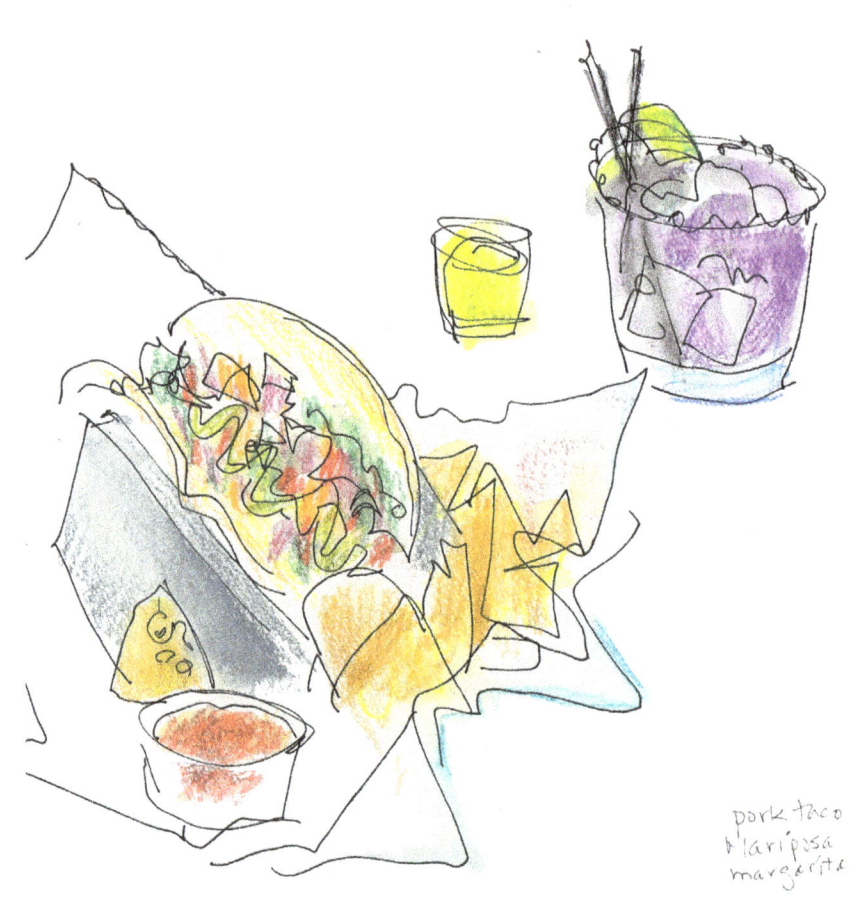

pork taco
Mariposa
margarita

Acknowledgments

Many thanks are due to many people in the creation of this book. The book's designer is my talented and patient daughter, Karin. Together we chose fonts, cover images and colors. Karin and Piscataqua Press then prepared the images for the printers in Nashville.

My late husband Bruce, in my previous books, expertly scanned the artwork, and did the proofreading too. We carry on in his memory. The encouragement and belief of my family and friends is always my anchor in my book projects and in life. Lastly, thank you to the Newmarket Historical Society for their many extensively researched articles about the town, posted online.

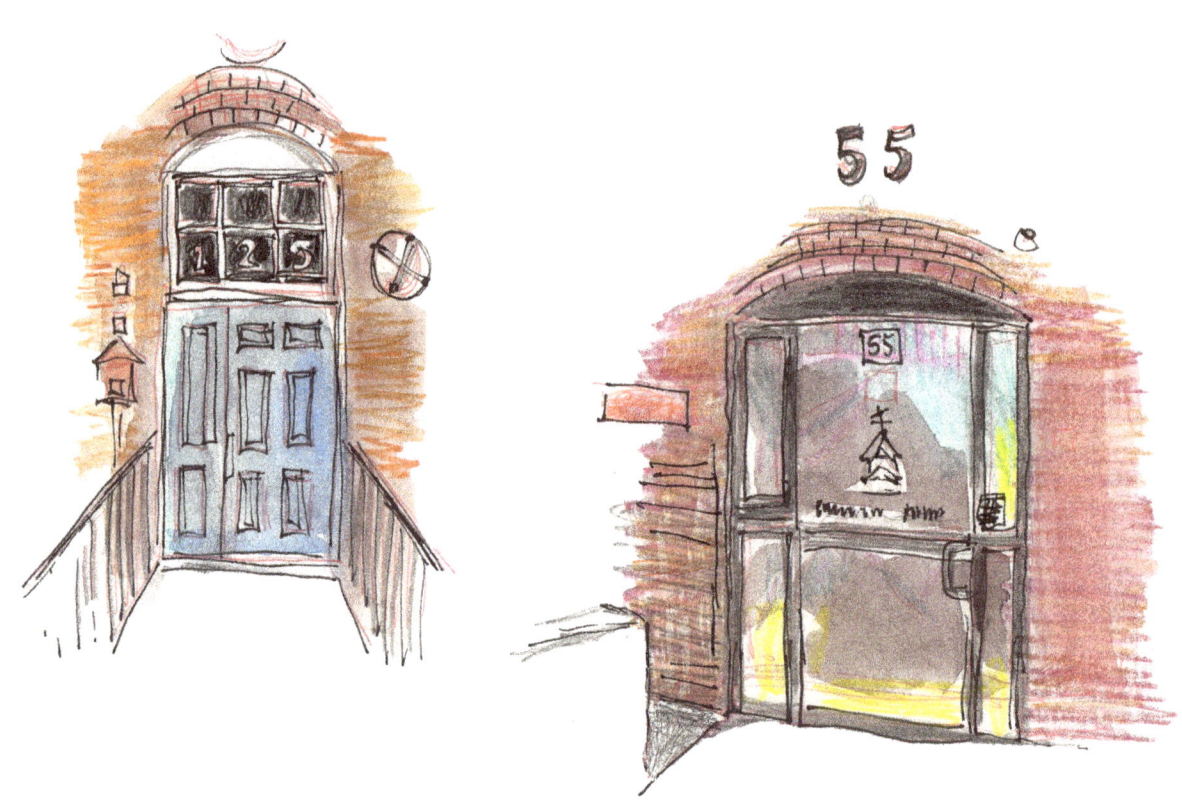

Previous Titles by the Artist-Author

Colorful Journey: An Artist's Adventure Drawing Every Town in New Hampshire, 2014

Pep Talks for the Would-Be, Should-Be Artist, 2016

A Small City by the Sea: An Artist's View of Portsmouth, New Hampshire, 2018

A Week Sketching in the Galapagos, 2020

A to Z New London, 2021

The New London Barn Playhouse Campus: A Construction Sketchbook, 2021-2022

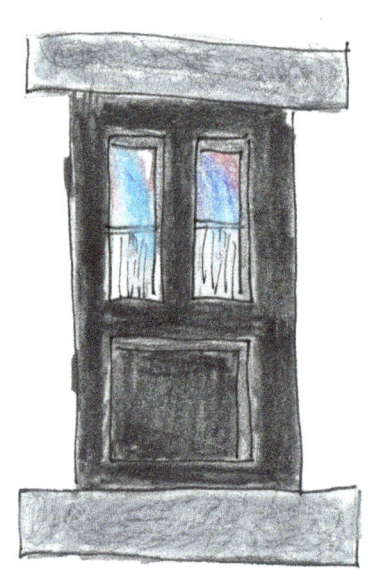

www.ingramcontent.com/pod-product-compliance
Lightning Source LLC
Chambersburg PA
CBHW052135170526
45162CB00003B/18